T0171389

AboutAverage.Com

My Internet Dating Debacle...

By: Jacey Hill

iUniverse, Inc.
New York   Bloomington

Copyright © 2010 by Jacey Hill

All rights reserved. No part of this book may be used or reproduced by any means,
graphic, electronic, or mechanical, including photocopying, recording, taping or by any
information storage retrieval system without the written permission of the publisher
except in the case of brief quotations embodied in critical articles and reviews.

iUniverse books may be ordered through booksellers or by contacting:

iUniverse
1663 Liberty Drive
Bloomington, IN 47403
www.iuniverse.com
1-800-Authors (1-800-288-4677)

Because of the dynamic nature of the Internet, any Web addresses or links contained in this book may
have changed since publication and may no longer be valid. The views expressed in this work are solely
those of the author and do not necessarily reflect the views of the publisher, and the publisher hereby
disclaims any responsibility for them.

ISBN: 978-1-4502-2999-9 (sc)
ISBN: 978-1-4502-3001-8 (hc)
ISBN: 978-1-4502-3000-1 (ebook)

Printed in the United States of America

iUniverse rev. date: 5/21/2010

Dedicated to Nannie ~ my angel, my inspiration
to find sweet love the second time around.

The Calm Before the Storm

It was a difficult time for me. I was in a lonely funk still trying to absorb the reality of my impending divorce. I was living a life that I thought belonged to some old maid who chose loneliness and cats over affection and companionship with an actual human being. Granted, I didn't have cats, in fact, I don't even care for cats due to their quiet sneakiness. And, I wasn't exactly lonely either. Not yet, anyway. I had my two children, my two parents, and my many friends. I was just sad and hurt and getting through life day by day. In my heart I felt young, in my mind I felt old, and in the mirror I felt ugly. No wonder I felt alone. The feelings I had about myself were isolated and nothing blended together anymore. That was lonely within myself.

Each day I rose, lethargically, out of the right side of the bed, still not daring to touch the left side. The left side was his side, my ex's side. It remained untouched and fully made every day, even after I had had a full night's sleep. Each day I rolled out of the right side, swinging my feet to the cream bedroom carpet, pulled and tightened the covers to make the bed and then off to the sweet bedrooms of a new baby and a chipper toddler.

These little girls were ready and eager to start their day every morning as if yesterday never happened. I wished I could to that. I would awake to the baby talking to herself in her crib, bed head sticking up in every direction. She would hear me in my bathroom brushing my teeth and hop up on her little feet, grab onto the crib railing and eagerly await my arrival. I would open the door slowly, gently peer in to see if she noticed me right away, and then we would lock eyes instantly. The first thing I would see was her dark, thick baby hair all over the place which caused me to hold back my initial giggles, but then I would see those baby blue eyes staring at me with the sleepy puff surrounding her lids, searching

1

for recognition. She would look at me and her smile would stretch as far across her face as she could stretch it, revealing a mouth of empty gums and two giant dimples denting the center of each cheek. Immediately, her reaction was to start jumping in her crib, smiling, and laughing to be lifted out into the new day. Walking closer to her and watching her try to balance on the unsteady mattress with her chubby feet while she attempted to raise her hands to me, I lifted her out of her crib, snuggled her sweet baby smell and kissed her from her velvet neck right into the depths of those dimples.

"Good morning, funny face", I would say in her little ear.

"How was your sleep"? I would ask as she batted me with excitement and nuzzle her kissy, drooling lips into my neck.

This was how she greeted every morning, most of the time. She greeted me with the innocence of baby, the security of mommy, and the happiness of the moment. At what point do we lose that in life? When do those magical qualities just vanish and disappear?

Next I would hear the little pitter patter of three year old feet running across a carpeted room. My senses were heightened every time I honed in on the footsteps of my sweet girl. My first born. She was the most angelic thing I had ever laid eyes on when she was born. Perfectly flawless skin with the glow and quiet peace of a newborn. A small tuft of light brown hair that didn't require primping until she was over a year old. A smile that encouraged twinkles of love and laughter in her rich, brown eyes. She was happy, smart, and friendly, surrounded by an aura of peace, sensibility, and reason. There were no temper tantrums, just unconditional open arms of love from this child. She, too, was comforted with the sense of security with mommy. She, too, was clueless of her parental surroundings that were filled with angst. She, too, eager to start her happy-filled day of whatever it had to offer. Every morning, my three year old would try to teach me to greet each day with new hope, minus the resentment, without ever realizing it. I believe her aura is surrounded by angels helping to guide her emotional mother.

I would stand and look over at the baby's bedroom door as I changed the early morning diaper of the day. There stood my toddler with that beautiful twinkly smile on her face. Her brown hair tousled by a peaceful nights sleep in her big girl bed, her flowing princess night gown that probably encouraged the sweetest dreams of castles and white knights, and the bare little feet with painted pink toenails, squishing into the plush bedroom carpet. Usually carrying a book, toy or a pruned thumb and blankey, she would hug me, kiss me, and greet her sister with all the unconditional love and innocence of a three year old.

"Good morning my sweet peach"! I would say

"Good morning, Mommy", she would reply with a sleepy smile.

"How was your sleep, Honey"?

"I slept good, Mommy. I had dreams. My bed is a mess, Mommy".

"That's okay", I would reply. "Mommy'll fix it in a bit".

This was the morning, every morning. The three of us, the quiet of the house without anybody walking through the front door, or the telephone ringing, or the cartoons blasting from Nickelodeon. Every morning, this was the calm before the storm for each day. Before the splattered baby food all over the floor and the million slobber-dried cheerios stuck to whatever the baby could get her hands to touch. Before brushing knots and tangles out of a toddlers hair for preschool, causing unwanted tears from a little girl who always seemed cheerful. Before the rush to get two little ones loaded up in the car and to preschool on time. Before the gym class I wanted to make so I didn't feel like such a fat ass anymore. Before the expected, but unwanted, arrival of my soon-to-be ex who would show up for a *brief* visit with the girls. Before the endless phone calls from my mother at home, my father at the office, my lawyer in the lion's den, and my friends from their cell phones, all wanting know to know, 'how I was *doing* today'. Really, it felt like Groundhog Day. *Again.*

Regardless of the obvious commotion all day, I was still wandering around in a daze. I attempted each day in a fog of astonishment, confusion, and self-pity. I was clearly surrounded by love and support from every angle, yet, I still felt terribly alone and I was convinced that my childhood fear was coming true. I was going to be the "Old Maid". I was going to be that dreaded card of the Old Maid, staring back at me from my hand, while my friendly opponent was going to get the happy ending. The Old Maid, rocking in her rocking chair, knitting booties for her cats or something. I hated knitting, almost as much as my dislike for cats!

I was so relieved when I met my husband 7 years ago, overcoming that fear of Old Maid-ism. I felt like I was showing the world *'See? I wasn't gonna be an Old Maid! Ha!'.* Now, I was just feeling betrayed and insecure. I was questioning everything about myself that I had always felt secure about in the past. There I was, wondering how the old Maid snuck up on me without my knowing. Was I not paying attention? Was I taking it for granted? Was I too consumed in what I thought was a perfect start to a perfect life? Was I a shitty wife after all? Maybe I wasn't cut out for it? All I knew was that I was waking up to these two precious gifts of children and I had to keep trudging along for their sake, whether I was going to be rocking and knitting or not.

Some smart-asses may have an opinion that 25 years old is too young to get married. I really didn't feel that way at the time. I had been living large as a single, party girl for quite some time before my engagement and I felt deep down inside that I was ready to settle down into marriage and start a family. When I met my husband at the age of 24, I felt elated and ecstatic about my future and I couldn't wait to walk down the aisle. I was tired of the endless summer weekends in the Hamptons, turning the bar scene upside down every time my friends and I walked in. I was tired of the same local scene all winter, exhausting the hot spots of twenty something establishments in the northern suburbs of New York. I wanted more. I wanted more security and companionship and less hang-over. I wanted more comfort and less skin-tight. I wanted a wedding, not a one night stand. I wanted children, not more friends of convenience. I wanted dinner parties, not clubbing meat markets. I wanted a change, and magically, it was standing right before me in a six foot two body with dark hair and loving eyes.

My parents had been going strong with a wonderful, solid marriage and I really wanted to turn out like them. They had experienced tremendous loss and still managed to keep it together while many would have just fallen apart. I grew up in sort of a "Beaver Cleaver" type household filled with family dinners, vacations, huge Thanksgivings, play dates, and family outings. I really felt that this was the type of life I wanted to emulate with my future husband and strive for a life that made mine such a happy one thus far, with the obvious exception of the loss of my brother.

No family should experience loss like that, yet I silently applauded my parents for getting through it day by day. That loss, no doubt, made me more vulnerable in my life and the urgent sense of settling down was surely prompted by experiencing something being taken away so forcefully, unexpectedly, and sadly. Naturally, I wanted to cling on to everything good and solid I felt in my life at the moment and start living out my dreams, something my brother never got to do. I was on a mission for him and for me. I planned on providing the family, the next generation for both of us and I was feeling very positive, laced with a small sense of melancholy about it.

My parents planned a beautiful wedding for us with all the gorgeous fixings of a high class affair. It took place in Greenwich, Connecticut with a guest list of 200. It was the basic fairytale wedding with the big poufy gown, the filet mignon, and the ornate flower arrangements that rose off the table in three foot vases. The DJ played all night while everyone danced right up until the end. My parents felt proud as all their friends and family watched them marry off their only daughter, their only child existing in *this* world. I felt very content and the chronic hives that I experienced all over my body for the previous six months were finally at bay. (A sign?)

My husband and I settled into our new, little, married life tucked into our first crappy apartment on a busy semi-city main street. The Beeline Bus stop was right outside our window, with strangers lurking about the litter, waiting for their ride to somewhere else. Housing projects were across the street in beat up brick buildings and our living room window had a circular crack that mildly resembled a bullet hole of some sort. We made it there through some of the summer, but as the weather became hot and humid, the garbage incinerator for the apartment made me want to puke on a daily basis. No, I wasn't pregnant yet but the smell was completely vile.

When we first found this apartment, I was thrilled because we did it on our own, or at least, I did something with my husband that my parents weren't involved in. I came from a very sheltered life with my parents and rarely did *anything* on my own without their help, advice, or money. I had never even lived apart from them with the exception of going to college.

After spending a few short months there, I hated it. I hated the noise across the street and the aim that the window hole had. I hated the bus and its fumes every half an hour. I hated looking out the window at city litter. I hated the smell of the hallway and the incinerator, but mostly, I hated the raunchy people upstairs that had animal sex every weekend morning for hours. Nothing like working at a busy restaurant into the wee morning hours, only to awaken to the sounds of thumping, grunting, and moaning from an entire floor above. I was a bitch. I was a princess. We moved.

We found a new apartment in the opposite direction from the restaurant his family owned which was large enough for the two of us and it only had two stories. It was a little off the beaten path for me and the town it was situated in was yet another dump. Luckily, the apartment bordered on another town that was quite pretty and where I felt I could spend more time in. In fact, it reminded me of the town I grew up in as a child. My husband and I were happy there. It was a roomy 1 bedroom apartment with a large kitchen, decent living room, and a huge bedroom. We were forming our lives together as a married couple and were beginning to discuss the possibility of starting a family. Baby talk was coming quickly after the honeymoon but I felt ready to embark on this journey. I loved him, I loved the outlook our life had, and I really wanted to be a young mom. We knew our apartment would be too small for a baby but we figured we would make it work for the first few months.

Soon enough I was pregnant. It seems, I merely *thought* about getting pregnant and I tested positive on the little pee stick. That seemed easy. Life was heading exactly the way I thought it was supposed to. Not that it's not subject to change in the Grand Master scheme of things, but I was pretty happy with the way in which it was moving.

During my 4th month of pregnancy, my beloved Nana passed away, which deeply saddened me to no end. She was my mom's mom. We were very close my entire life and I just wanted her to hang in there to meet her great grandchild, but I guess she couldn't hold out any longer. I said my peaceful goodbyes and sent along my endless love. At that deeply sad moment, I would have never truly understood how much I would need her in the near future. If anyone was needed and longed for most, it was my Nannie. My Nana had been divorced early on in her first marriage back in the 40's when *divorce* was basically *unheard* of. My Grandpa was a player to some extent, at least that's *my* understanding. My Nana took on the lone responsibility of raising my mother while working multiple jobs and putting herself through school. In order to accomplish all of this, she made the difficult decision to enroll my 4 year old mother in a Catholic boarding school in lower Westchester at the time. My Nana was a single, working mother in the 1940's, and making life happen. She was smart, she was motivated, and she was living. I would have loved to know more of the details of that time in her life, but during the time of her passing, I would have never known to ask. Now, I just ask her every night in the dark and try to imagine the answers she would give me.

After Nannie died, my husband and I made the decision to move into her quiet condo, closer to where I grew up. It was a lovely condo complex with our unit nestled into the back woods. It was a nice sized 1 bedroom with 1 and a half bathrooms and a small den off the living room.

Every day, I came to enjoy and appreciate the sun peering through the trees from the dining room window, just as Nannie did for so many years before, while sipping her tea and doing her New York Times crossword puzzle. I, of course, didn't drink tea, and couldn't possibly get one single question right in The Times puzzle, but I enjoyed the quiet view just the same. Our new home offered us more room and a separate little space to bring a baby home to, which we did. Nannies' place offered us security, warmth, long walks, and proximity to Mimi and Pops (my parents), which is exactly what Nannie gave me my whole life and would have wanted for us and our new baby.

Over the next two years, I became easily accustomed to motherhood with a beautiful baby girl. We eventually bought a house nearby, owned a popular restaurant, and got ready for another baby. I was feeling excited about my life. I was putting a new home together, decorating a nursery, and all the while, feeling really proud of my husband and his booming business.

Our next daughter came in the early hours of a cold, January morning. She was round, pink, and had a full head of dark hair. *Two girls.* Wow, something I would surely have to get used to. I knew nothing about sisters but I hoped, right then and there, that these two precious girls would be as close as two could be. I hoped they would share friendship, love, trust, and a deep connection that I really was clueless about without having a sister.

I had a brother and we were very different. We had different temperaments, different talents, different interests, and different experiences. We were as close as a brother and sister could be while growing up through childhood but we didn't really become close until just before he died. We had found that friendship, that trust, that love, and that deep connection. Then in an instant, it was stolen away by a horrific car accident on a rainy morning. I prayed that my daughters would know this type of relationship early on, because secretly, I know not to waste a single moment. I was elated, excited, and ready to take on motherhood, family hood, house hood, and, now, sisterhood. All in all, I had a family in tact, a roof over our heads, a successful business, and healthy parents. Was that the calm before the storm or what! Always a storm on the horizon….

"I didn't sleep with her", he stated matter of factly in the dampness of the garage while smoking a cigarette.

"We just hooked up a couple of times", he continued as if that would make it sound better.

"WHO"? was all I could muster up.

"Just someone I met at the restaurant. She's been coming in lately. She's from Pelham."

"Are you leaving me? We have a brand new baby upstairs! Are you *leaving me?*"

"I don't know what I want. Not her, though, if that's what you think."

Great, I wasn't sure what was worse; getting left for someone or getting left for no one!

"How many times"? I demanded.

"Twice".

I nodded for lack of anything better to do. Once, twice, ten times. It didn't matter. The damage was done. But, with every ounce of strength I had, I threw him backwards into the garage door. It *still* didn't matter. The damage was *still* done.

The storm had hit. Since the story is not really about my marriage, I won't delve any deeper than to say that when my youngest was about 6 weeks old I received my marital pink slip at the Outback Steakhouse, simply stating that my husband had apparently "changed his mind" about being married. Huh? Surprise was an understatement, confusion was incomprehensible, and hurt was beyond painful. And, I've never returned to the Outback Steakhouse again. Kudos to him for picking a public place where I couldn't truly freak out!

Okay, married, two kids, and divorced by thirty. Not exactly what I signed up for while walking down the aisle of my fancy Greenwich wedding.

Gunpoint

I knew I had to get "out there". I had to get off my butt and get back into the dating scene, except I was crying all the time, and confused about how I was supposed to "meet" people.

"Join a singles group", my mom would say.

"Go into the city", my mom would say.

"Try the online dating", my mom would say.

I wasn't going for any of it. I felt scared, humiliated, discarded, scared, confused, nervous, and anxious. Did I mention scared? Well, I was. I was scared to walk into a room full of unknown single people because I didn't know what I was walking into. You can call it a cooking class or a hike across a mountain, or give out free drinks, but everyone involved knows that it's a single thing, you know, just "getting to know people". I don't think it's as simple as that for anyone, and certainly not for me. I consider myself to be a fairly outgoing girl with an education and a sense of humor but no "single" circumstance will ever be easy to just join or walk into!

Funny, I could make a friend under a rock, in an elevator, or online at CVS. I *was* an outgoing person. I *knew* this. I never lacked for friends or connections. I knew that if I was thrust into one of those single situations, I could probably handle it, maybe meet a new friend or make a connection. I was just embarrassed. I felt like a failure. I couldn't even reach the five year milestone of my marriage without him straying, which of course made me question my looks, my sexuality, and my future. My confidence felt shattered in every nook of my being, and I was feeling too frightened to even step out on a limb and open up the possibility of a single environment. Maybe what I needed was a single-mommy-therapy group for women barely thirty years old.

Every time I thought I had my head wrapped around what happened and thought I could try to move one, I started to wonder if it would happen again. If the next person would stray. If the next person would leave. If the next person would fall out of love. Or, my never ending fear; would the next person just wake up and change his mind, too. I couldn't help wondering what I did to cause this.

Getting back on my single feet was nearly impossible. I felt like a baby foal wobbling all over four new legs, trying to find some balance, stability, or maybe just someone to lean on. Knowing my husband had given me the ultimate rejection, I was still sporting post-partum weight, and let's not forget two babies attached at my hip, I had a feeling this wasn't going to be one of my easiest tasks in life. Cruel joke? I think so because every morning my brain woke up to the silent laughing in my ear before my eyes had even opened. Cruel joke? I think no. I think very real. So that's a synopsis of how I found myself in this online debacle of internet dating. Considering what I had just experienced with my so-called husband, how could the computer be any worse? Really.

Finally, at one of my lowest points, I found myself frantically typing a profile on a singles website for dating, with my mother breathing down my neck from behind. It felt like she had a gun pointed in the small of my back. My mother didn't want any more excuses from me, including the one where I tried to convince her that dating online was too expensive for someone in my financial predicament.

"I'll pay for it" she replied as she whipped out her credit card.

"Mom", I whined, "I feel *stupid* having you and dad pay for this. *This* is stupid. *I* feel stupid about this. *Please*.", I begged.

"No. Nope. You're doing this right now, while I'm here. Enough is enough!" my mother stated.

"Fine", I sighed with a partial whine. I felt *stupid*.

Hmmm, no excuses now. In fact, I was out of them. The truth was, there was no real good reason for me not to try the online dating thing. So, I typed a profile. Of course I found myself scared to death again. Not only was I going through a series of major life changes at 30 years old with two babies, but now I was expected to put personal information into the computer *with* a picture *and* date the strangers!

I barely dated anyone before I got married! In fact, I didn't even know how to date! *What do you say? Where do you meet? Do you meet or does he pick you up? Who pays? Do you go out to eat or do you go out for drinks? What does a lady order for a drink? Beer or wine? Am I even considered a lady or a girl or a chick or a mom or what? Do you talk about how you met? Do you talk about why you're on the damn website? What are people wearing these days on dates? Should I tell my friends where I am in case he's a psycho? Should I just tell them to call or text me anyway? Should I plan on meeting up with friends afterwards? Do I have to kiss him hello or goodbye? Do I tell people the truth in case I run into someone I know?* Oh, the questions were torturing me, but my mother breathing down the back of my neck was worse! So, I typed.

A profile. A single profile. A single mother profile. I spent an hour clicking on generic things of interest like music, books, movies, blah, blah. I clicked on generic appearances like brown eyes, auburn hair, and an 'about average' body. I clicked on some of my favorite things like the beach, food, blah, blah. I clicked on my marital status and my kid status like separated, widowed, divorced and how many kids I have. I clicked away with my exercise routines, my amount of drinking and smoking, my political views, and my salary. I clicked on generic things I'm looking for in a man like, height, body type, hair, eyes, education, and marital/kid status. I basically clicked myself into oblivion. The deep, dark hole of the internet that holds all my personal, sacred information and will magically find me a match! Hilarious, but my mom was still there so I kept typing.

The words "about average" kept sticking in my brain like a wad of gum on the bottom of my shoe on a hot day. I couldn't shake it off, scrape it away, or break free from the cling that those words had on me. About average? *Was I? I suppose.* Looking around the imaginary world of my computer room, becoming divorced was about average when keeping in mind the current marital statistics in the world. Being a single mom was about average, as I have been coming across in the local parks and school yards. Being a size 12 was about average, seeing as though I can never seem to find my size on the racks. Being a teacher is considered an about average career by most standards, unless you're a teacher and know you are shaping the young minds of America. But, really, no pressure. So, yeah, I guess "about average" pretty much described me, considering the way my life was shaping up to be.

It was finally time to type freely and say what you want to say. It didn't have to be generic or be any particular length. I wanted to be my witty self but I couldn't figure out how to type that way in a situation that I didn't even want to be in the first place. I wanted to have charm and humor, but lace it with a sweetness or an innocence representing how uncomfortable I was with this. I wanted to be desirable and sexy, but that's hard to get across in a profile allowing so many "characters". In fact, had I gone that route, I probably would have been the one who *sounded* like a character! Instead, I just kept it real and honest, but safe. To me, safe means not necessarily disclosing too much information about ones private life. Call it shy, call it cautious, or call it walls because that's what I had surrounding me! I felt guarded and wasn't feeling too keen on letting anyone in just yet.

When I finally finished typing, and I was paid up with a screen name and a password, I think my mom felt satisfied enough to leave. I was in the computer with an official profile. I was about to embark on online dating. God help me.

I found it difficult concentrating because I was already starting to stress about posting my photo. I mean, what kind of photo do you post of yourself? I guess an attractive one but I felt absolutely ridiculous searching my own photos for myself. Not to mention that most of the photos of me are usually with my arm around one of my friends or my kids. So, I did some searching, cropping, some shifting, and some final decision making, choosing one that I thought I looked pretty okay in. Still, the idea of my photo floating around for all to see was a little nerve racking.

It's at this moment in time when someone's self-esteem and confidence are truly put to the test, to be more specific, mine. More questions flooded my brain like *what if I wasn't pretty enough? What if I didn't look like my photo? What if my mouth is too big? Or if I wear too much make-up? What if my arms look fat? What if they can see my friend or my kid? What if I change my hairstyle?* More questions, more personal torture. I figured I was safe now that my mom had left, so I decided to hold off on the picture thing for the first couple of weeks and see what happened. I thought I would use that time to "get used" to the online idea and find the perfect picture of myself, but I think every woman knows that there is no "perfect picture" of yourself, unless you're a model and have been airbrushed in all the right places. We seem to find fault in every picture, but I did my best. For my mother.

I basically avoided this new website in my life, letting the idea of my public profile marinate in my brain. I waited a couple of weeks for the official picture posting like I had planned and began to check my new website companion daily…. just to see. It seemed that many people were looking at me even though I hadn't put a photo on yet but the strangers looking at my personal information were a bit discouraging. These people, although clearly not shallow (because of my lacking photo) were definitely not the type of people I would embark on a date with. Some were much older than I, and could probably hang out with my dad instead. Some were not as educated as I would have preferred and sometimes spelling *does* count (at least for the small words). Some were clearly "players" and "serial daters". I have had plenty of experiences with the bad boys of the world and the good- looking ones too, but I wasn't emotionally ready for either of those types at this moment of my life.

As far as I am aware in the dating world, a "player" is usually someone who looks good, acts smooth, and charms the pants off of you….literally. I suppose if one is looking to get a little laid and seems not to care about more than that, maybe a player is the right choice for the evening. Mostly, though, they are typically looking for some arm candy for the evening, aka, someone that looks *almost* as good as them, standing by their side for all to see. I was never petite enough to be this kind of date!

A "serial dater" apparently goes on dates with anyone and everyone just to make it clear to the world that they *are* dating. I have heard that quite a few suburban moms have been known to serial date, basically to try to stick it to their ex and seem as though they are out and about, having a grand old time. I have never found it necessary to do this and will probably remain this way. As I'm sure some of these men staring at me from the computer screen were very nice and trying to lead normal lives, they just weren't my "type". Even if they were my type, I'm not quite sure I fell into the serial dater type just yet. Anyway, what was my type? Who knew at that point, but I was pretty sure it was none of my new hits.

It's funny, because when my profile was hit on and people viewed me, it was like the equivalent of getting hit on in a bar except there were *so* many more hits online! Not bad for one's struggling self-esteem. As I became more comfortable with my new situation, I began to browse. I would curl up in my dark red leather office chair and…browse. When one browses online, it's like internet shopping for style, color, and size!

Hmmm, I'll take one with brown hair, maybe with a slight curl, straight teeth, preferably an intoxicating smile, at least five foot eleven. Gimme the one with the confident attitude and maybe the solid job. No crazy ex-wife, but a couple of kids would be fine. Pack that up, ship it to my address, and charge it to my card! Wait for internet confirmation!

Of course, then it dawned on me that that was what people were doing to me and my profile. It was that enlightening moment when I realized that I really *need* my photo posted, no matter *how* I criticized myself. The bottom line was, I, at least have to know what in the world I'm browsing or shopping for and, therefore, so do they! So I dug out the little photo that I chose of myself and… uploaded. The final test of my courage, at least in this stage of the game! I was so nervous about running into people I knew through thumbnail photos. I was petrified to receive messages from old acquaintances wondering, 'what are *you* doing on here?' I had fears of people whispering about me in public because they recognized me from the internet. However, I knew what had to be done and I thought it would be interesting to see if there was a shift in my admirers. So I got over my nerves, posted the photo, and waited to see if the results would get better. Not a lot better, but better. At least they knew who they were looking at now and I knew who I was looking at which made it more of a fair game on this new found website that entered my life at God speed.

So I clicked and browsed, clicked and browsed, entered zip codes, mileage, and clicked and browsed some more. I tried to keep it fairly local at first but then I started feeling a little gutsy and began entering zip codes for Manhattan and Connecticut.

Eventually, I received an email. I wasn't sure what to do with it. Initially, I was so shocked to see an alert for a new message. It was like receiving a letter in the mail without a return address. You want to tear it open and check out what's inside, but first you force yourself to turn it around, hold it up to the light, and inspect the handwriting. I couldn't really do that with this kind of mail. I just stared at the alert. The obvious choice was to open it but that would have made the whole mysterious adventure come to life, so I thought about it. I figured I went through all the trouble of clicking away a fairly decent profile, got up enough courage to upload my photo, and now I'm actually browsing….what the hell- I opened it and responded.

Contestant #1

For the sheer protection of privacy for my dates, I will refer to them as contestants which seems apropos, considering the whole thing was like being in the middle of some weird, internet game show. Here you are trying to beef yourself up in a limited, poorly- typed profile, with only so many characters allowed, a thumbnail picture to spruce it up and clearly represent you, while being gazed at and browsed upon.

"What do we have behind curtain #1?"

"Well, Bob, we have this lovely redhead with an 'about average' body, brown eyes, and two kids! She loves reading and writing and watching movies. She is recently divorced and has no idea what the hell she's doing on this website!"

"And behind curtain #2?"

"Behind curtain #2, Bob, we have a curvy blonde who likes horses and smokes occasionally. She loves to party and date a variety of guys with different interests. She hasn't found her special someone yet so she is giving this a whirl!"

"And #3?"

"Bob, behind #3 is a tall brunette who likes hikes and bikes! She wants to settle down and have two to three babies immediately due to the ticking of her biological clock."

I guess we're all contestants in this game show, so I don't feel bad referring to my dates as such.

So, back to Contestant #1. He seemed to be nice looking, from what I could tell in the 1 inch by 1 inch frame. Basic blonde hair, combed back and off to the side, with light, blue-eyes. He was tall, maybe about six foot three, which I liked, although not imperative. God knows I have been with my share of petite men throughout the years. Actually, it felt kind of nice to have the presence of a tall man around me again.

I just love a good presence, although I don't believe that height creates presence. Presence is something that's invisible and comes with either a quiet confidence or a strong personality. Presence can really come in any size, but I have to feel it to know it. It often feels very attractive to me, sometimes even protective. In this case, it was the quiet confidence in a taller man. *Whatever.*

Anyway, Contestant #1 seemed nice enough and easy to talk to. While we began to chat away on the phone, he acted genuinely interested in me and my baggage, although I tried not to reveal too much and scare my first Contestant off. *And,* I hate to even refer to parts of my life using the word "baggage", but going through a divorce, having lawyers in your life, and one extremely large commitment to two very small children could be considered baggage to some and I figured I would use the universal language of the new statistics! I prefer the phrase "package deal" instead but the word '*deal*' might be debatable for some. In fact, some might consider my 'package deal' to be a total 'deal *breaker*' instead!

Contestant #1 shared custody of a little girl with his ex, so at least so far, we had that in common.

"She is the love of my life and I have her every Wednesday and every other weekend", he explained to me.

"That must be hard to wait that long to see her in between that amount of time", I added.

"Oh it is. It kills me. What's your visitation schedule like?" he asked.

"Well, my ex is in the restaurant business so weekends are really not an option for him at this time. He pretty much sees them a little bit almost every day and has 1 sleepover midweek."

"That's weird. You have to see him almost every day?" he asked.

"Yeahhhh. It's not always easy because I don't always feel like looking at him, speaking with him, or dealing with him on an everyday basis. I guess it's good for my girls though. At least they get plenty of face time with him and I won't interfere with that."

"You're right about that. I miss my little girl when I'm not with her and the time between sure does go by slowly. I just love her to death."

She was little, around the age of 3 or 4 which is what I was in the midst of in my own home. We were able to have smooth communication about our daughters due to our similar circumstances of divorce and the fact that our girls were roughly around the same age.

As far as I can remember, because it was some time ago, he was some sort of computer guy which immediately made me feel idiotic, seeing as though I can barely retrieve my email half the time. In fact, I was still trying to figure out the ins and outs of the dating website. Now I had two places to check for emails and messages, which can really screw up a girl experiencing technical difficulties. He was a guy who fixed things within a computer, so maybe he could be the perfect match for me after all!

"So you work with computers, right?" I asked.

"Yes, I've always been really into the technology stuff so people call upon me at work to fix all their screw ups and computer glitches. I like it because it's kind of like a puzzle to me and I'm determined to fit all the pieces together".

"I could never do something like that. I have no patience for computers and don't even know where to start when something goes wrong." I add.

"Well, that's why I do what I do! To help people like you!" he laughed.

Since our conversations were going so smoothly through the phone lines, we planned to meet for our first date and have lunch at TGI Fridays, which seemed safe enough seeing as though it was lunchtime, there would be no drinking alcoholic beverages, and it was broad daylight. It was a convenient spot to meet, falling in a middle location between where I lived and where he worked. I really was very nervous. My stomach was fluttering, my hands were a little clammy, and my head was swirling. All the questions I had been questioning myself with were spinning in my head and I still hadn't come up with any answers, which I knew wouldn't ever happen unless I put myself out there on these dates.

I began answering the questions I had asked myself by planning to meet him at Fridays. Actually, two question solved; a) that we should *meet*. b) a location. So, two issues solved. Then I had to figure out what was appropriate to wear for a lunch date, or any date for that matter.

I stood in front of my closet staring at clothes that were severely questionable at this point. I was not equipped with dating material clothing. I was equipped with mommy clothing, gym clothing, and whatever else fit! I hadn't really begun to give a crap yet about fitting into my new environment of single land because I was still worried about fitting into anything post-pregnancy! I continued to stare into the deep, dark, closet of nothing flattering and grabbed a few staple items, threw them onto my bed and arranged them as though there were a body beneath them.

Becoming frustrated with my lack of variety and choices, I took a break from arranging and wandered into the bathroom to do my hair and make-up. At least these two aspects of myself hadn't changed too much. I had already grown out of the recent perm that I mistakenly allowed myself after my husband left. Just a little blow dry and it was as straight as it could be. Maybe that perm was the first of many mistakes following a separation. Upon his leaving, I wasn't sure where I fit in. Immediately, I reverted back to pre-marriage and what I looked like before walking down the aisle. I'm not really sure that was the direction to head but I was so lost and confused to find myself that I thought a new direction *on* my head was the answer. It was not! It was old, not new. Now it was straight, thank God!

I finished my hair and make-up and returned to the edge of my bed where my scattered choices laid, somewhat arranged into an outfit. I got dressed in a final decision and stretched and peered in front of the mirror to try to check out every angle I had. Satisfied that what I was seeing was as good as it was going to get for the time being, I gathered up my little "package deals", loaded them into their car seats, and I dropped them off at my mom's.

"Oooo, don't you look nice", she said to me upon opening the kitchen door to help me in with the girls.

"Thanks" I replied unenthusiastically.

"What's the matter? I think you look very classy and casual. Take your coat off and turn around" she said.

"Ugh, Mom" I semi-whined. "Fine", I added as I reluctantly removed my heavy coat.

She checked me and my outfit out from head to toe and back up again and gave me an eye twinkle of approval. I eventually had made the decision to dress in a pair of jeans, low-heeled boots, and a simple sweater that didn't reveal too much. Since it was chilly, I had my big leather coat to cuddle into for security and belted around my waist. I didn't look like anything extravagant but I didn't feel frumpy either. Just casual and safe.

"I think you look very nice", my mom stated very matter of factly.

Then I hit the road. As I drove to our expected destination I thought, *'more questions'! Would he look like his picture? Was this a set-up and maybe this website was a bunch of bullshit? What would I order to eat? Would he think I looked like my photo? How would we recognize each other?* Torture. I continued to feel butterfly-ish, clammy, and swirly but I was determined to do it and get through it, dammit!

I found him. *Thank God.* It wasn't that hard because it *was* lunchtime *and* broad daylight, as previously planned. We met in the waiting area of the restaurant where the front foyer is and the nice hostess comes from inside and hold open the door for you. We greeted each other politely with an innocent peck on the cheek. He bent down toward me as I attempted to reach my face up a little. No tippy toes were required due to my heeled boots.

Contestant #1 seemed to be exactly what his profile and picture portrayed so my worries ceased a little. Only a little. He *was* tall, he *was* blonde, he *still* had light blue eyes just like his tiny little profile picture. We sat at an open table covered in a red and white striped tablecloth which was the signature décor for Fridays. We ordered and munched on appetizer foods and sipped a couple of sodas before he had to head back to work. Not bad. The conversation went well and we learned a little more about each other than what the profiles gave away. We spoke about our kids, our visitation, and the reason for our divorces. I didn't feel too uncomfortable but the sense of pressure always lingered over my head like a storm cloud. I was never really too proud to reveal the reason for my divorce, but I was a crappy liar so I came clean. The bottom line? We were all searching the internet for someone to accept our unfortunate personal situations and, some, were actually more fucked up than mine! So far his situation seemed as normal as one's divorce might be, however this *was* my first date and I had nothing to compare it to. He *was* very nice *and* polite *and* well-mannered *and* nice looking. That's all I knew at that point. I survived.

After our lunch date, Contestant #1 and I bid each other goodbye with a friendly handshake and another polite peck on the cheek. I guess that was all that was expected of me so we headed off separately to our cars. When I plopped myself in the drivers seat, I let out a big exhale, like I had just climbed Mt. Everest and made it back down the mountain in one piece. I tried to peer out the corner of my eye to see what kind of car he was getting into but I couldn't catch a visual. In fact, I couldn't see his tall build at all so I was concluding that he wasn't a lingering weirdo.

I was feeling pretty okay as I slipped my sunglasses on in bright winter sunlight. The butterflies had all disappeared, the dryness erased the clamminess in my soft hands, and the swirling ceased in my head as I began to clearly go over all the details of our date. As I drove, I reflected on the last hour and a half on my way back to my mom's to pick up the kids. Along the drive, I was feeling pretty relieved and pretty damned proud of myself. I went on my first internet date! Yay! But why did I still feel like such an awkward loser? It was sort of an unfinished feeling, like I just gave an estimate or put in a bid to a client and I'd have to hear back from them as to whether or not I got the job. *Would I hear back from this guy? Did I sell myself strong enough to get the job?* Unfinished. Unfinished, awkward loser!

Of course, upon my arrival at my mother's, she insisted to know every little detail, which I relayed as best I could.

"He was nice looking, Mom. He has blonde hair, blue eyes, and he's pretty tall".

"What else? How did he act?"

"He was really nice. Ya know, he had nice manners and was polite and pretty gentle. We talked about a lot of things that we mostly talked about on the phone already, but that's okay".

"Well, did you have a big lunch? Drinks?" she prodded.

"No, actually we got a few appetizers to share and we drank soda. Nothing crazy, Mom. Really".

"So how did you two leave it?" she let linger out in awkward land.

"Umm, he shook my hand, gave me a peck on the cheek, and said he would call me. Who knows! All I care about at this point is that I made it through *a* date in *one* piece. I mean, it would be *nice* if he called me but I have no idea how the date went in *his* mind so I dunno."

Being that she was quite familiar with the way these profiles were set up, seeing as though she watched every word I typed when I created mine, she was expecting every last detail disclosed in the middle of her dining room. After I filled her in the best to my ability she relented, deciding it sounded pretty promising.

"Well I hope he is he going to call you"

"We'll see", I responded in an empty-I-doubt-it kind of way.

"Well, did he *say* he was going to call you"?

"I mean, did he *seem* interested in you"?

I thought she was relenting…apparently not.

"Did he mention whether or not he'd like to see you again?"

"Yes, he said he would call. I thought he seemed interested. No, he didn't *actually* say whether or not he wanted to see me again. We'll see."

Although it was my mother who got me into this potential mess in the first place, I also had to remember that she, herself, hadn't been on a date in quite a long time. Maybe 30+ years to be exact.

"Ya know honey, in *my* day we didn't have cell phones or answering machines. In *my* day we had to *wait* for the guy to call and sometimes it took for-*ever*! When I was dating your father, he would take *weeks* to call me again!"

"Hopefully he liked you enough to call back a little sooner than your father did." She added.

Ahhh, my first date and I didn't die. My mother might kill me but the date didn't. In fact, I *was* going to see him again because he *did* call and he *was* interested in seeing me again! We decided to go out in the evening like most normal adults do! So far, Contestant #1 wasn't so bad!

The following weekend, we planned another date. We met in front of a bar that we were mutually familiar with in my home town. Another one of my previous, worrisome questions had been answered. I wasn't thrilled about the idea of going into that particular bar because I hadn't been in there in over 15 years due to its stale smell and seedy crowd. All is good when you're in your early 20's and stuff like that doesn't matter. Not now. Anyway, I pulled up into the parking lot across the street, ready to park, when I spotted him sitting in the small car beside me. Since I saw that he was waiting there first, I got out of my car, he got out of his car and we greeted each other with a peck on the cheek. And, yet, another previous question answered.

"Hi", he said. "You look great".

"Thanks" I responded, hesitantly looking down and recalling what I was wearing. I guess he had meant my face looked great because he couldn't possibly see what I was wearing yet underneath my big, black leather coat.

"Why don't you jump in then and we can get going." He said to me.

This was a question that hadn't even popped into my head. I never even entertained the thought of getting into a strangers car. Everything from the year I was 15 years old burst back into my memory. *You are not allowed to get into ANY cars, I don't care who it is, where you're going, or how long they've had their license. The answer is NO!* I can't remember if that was my mom or dad's voice but that's irrelevant because they both said and felt the same way, give or take a couple words. Then I heard my *own* mommy voice whispering *stranger danger, stranger danger* . I had to get into my moment and remind myself that I was a grown woman trying to live life on my own. I needed to stop letting my brain overreact. Besides, everyone I knew was kept up to date of my plans. I had even given the guys phone number to my friend just in case! Some might think that's a little extreme but my brain *was* whispering *stranger danger* so maybe it wasn't too crazy after all.

I decided to make a grown-up decision to get in his car. I figured it was his car or the seedy bar. *Bar or car? Maybe just a double-edged sword. Car, I guess.*

It was a nice car, a Saab or something like that. It was clean, it was close, and it was fast! The guy drove like a freaking lunatic to the point that I have absolutely no recollection of where we went. In fact, he drove so fast, that besides the dotted white lines appearing like a total blur on the highway, the night zipped right by and I found myself back in the parking lot of the bar we originally met at. Obviously he hadn't made that much of an impression on me during the second date or maybe I just never got past the part of the *stranger danger* thing. He wasn't actually dangerous yet, I just think maybe he wasn't that impressionable.

We pulled back into the familiar parking lot in across from the old seedy bar. We sat there. *Now what?* Second date, its dark, we're alone. *Now what?* No moves were being made and I wasn't too upset by that. There were a few nervous smiles exchanged across the seats and minimal eye contact in the dark car. I couldn't actually figure out if I was attracted to the guy or not. I mean, he was nice looking and he was nice enough, but I just wasn't feeling it. My heart was thumping but I think it was nerves due to lack of anything to say at that point. Maybe it was due to his expectations that I wasn't aware of. I knew I didn't have much desire to lean the car seat backwards and get busy. I didn't even have the desire to lean in for anything. Clearly, I just didn't have the desire. He had the desire, though. The desire for something else, apparently.

"Wanna smoke some weed?" he said within the dark car.

The words, any words at that point, sliced through the silence like a sharp knife through a ripe watermelon.

"Huh?" I eloquently replied.

"Weed. Pot. Do you get high?" he clarified.

"Well, I have. I mean, I occasionally do with friends in the confines of someone's house. That's it", I explained. I was stumped.

Why I felt the need to explain myself was totally beyond me, but I felt like that was the mature thing to do rather than freak out, look at him like he had two heads, and slam out of the car. I wasn't sure if I was insulted because he wanted to smoke pot on our first date or that he wanted to smoke pot rather than make a bold move on me. I knew I did not have the desire to be with him but it would have been nice to *be* desired! I clarified my feelings a little more, adding a polite edge mixed with an aloof attitude.

"No thanks."

Then he looked at me in that stumped sort of way.

I'm not really sure when it was that I exited the car and said good bye because I was too busy concentrating on the set of balls he had to suggest getting high with me on our first nighttime, adult date. *My first time adult date!* I love a good giggle with the stuff but I was hoping for a little more class for my first date. *I don't think so.* Contestant #1 is over.

Notes to self:
No 1st date should *ever* suggest smoking pot.
Follow date in your *own* car!

Contestant #2

Feeling a little discouraged from the pot-smoking, computer speedster, I went back online to see if there were any new prospects. I kept wondering if this was the crap that was in store for me but I tried to push those thoughts out of my mind and keep an optimistic outlook. I mean, I really wanted to give this online thing a fair chance. Giving up too soon would only drive my mother's insistence further, and who knows where that would lead. She might have me booked on some European singles getaway! I brushed off the first experience like eraser shavings on a rough draft. I tried it out, kept some info, edited some info, and saved it in my files for the next Contestant.

So, was there a Contestant #2? Low and behold, there was! I couldn't really make out the guys picture too clearly, but the gist of it seemed alright. I mean, he looked like he had brown hair and brown eyes and no facial hair. A thumbnail photo holds a lot of mystery which can be good or bad. I figured, as long as I could make out some details like hair or eye color, maybe the photo was okay enough. True I tend to bend my head in every direction and squint at the computer screen for some self assurance. By his profile description, he seemed to have a good job. I believe it was some sort of marketing job in the city. I was never quite clear on the "marketing" job because it sounds more like an umbrella term for what could be a thousand types of jobs. Hey, it was a job and so far it wasn't in a restaurant. Okay, I'll bite.

I responded to Contestant #2 after he wrote me a simple note of 'hi, how ya doin' and we continued to email a bit over the next few days. He was very chatty, presumably with much to talk about so I wasn't feeling worried about any conversation lulls. Conversation lulls often worried me because I didn't want to be the non-stop talker out of sheer nervousness and bore the contestants to death, yet, I didn't want to be the non-talker who did all the listening and bored the contestants to death. I wasn't quite sure if I was boring Contestant #2 by not talking much, however, he never led on that he was bored but, rather, interested.

We decided to meet for drinks at a restaurant down the street from my house. I didn't mind the location, considering my last experience, but I wasn't thrilled about doing this in my hometown. I live in a small, village-type town where many people know many people and I *always* run into someone I know. I did it anyway just so I could try to enjoy date #2. At least we wouldn't be racing down the highway on this date, watching the blurred lines of the road from the window. Also, the location was so close to my house, it could be an easy escape if necessary.

It was a night time meeting so I was able to feel a little more prepared to get dressed for a date, rather than the lunchtime meeting. I decided to stick with what worked and put on my good, safe jeans that weren't too tight and not too loose. I put on black, comfortable heeled boots and a black, v-neck sweater. I liked the v-neck because it exposes enough skin to eliminate me as a prude, yet hide the cleavage enough to eliminate me as a slut. I also found that the night time dates enabled me to put on a darker lipstick and smoke up my eyes a little more, which always gave me the feel-good-and-slightly-sexy feeling. All in all, I felt like I was dressed fairly simple and casual in an outfit that enhanced my average figure and complimented things I *wanted* complimented in one's mind.

After one more quick check in the mirror, leaning backwards and to the side to try to get a better glimpse of my ass, I realized this was as good as it was going to get. I through my coat on and was suddenly looking forward to a nice glass of red wine and someone new to meet. I jumped in the car and drove the 45 seconds down the road to the tiny place.

When I walked into the restaurant, which happened to be extremely small, we spotted each other right away. The place was located on the corner of two streets with a tiny, intimate dining room and a glass partition separating the bar. I walked in a little timidly, trying to focus in on the crowd while I was entering so that I didn't walk right in and stand there staring into a bunch of strangers wondering eyes. Luckily, I found him immediately because there was a non-existent crowd there during the winter on a week night.

Contestant #2 was occupying the only barstool in the bar, while the rest were left for empty. As soon as he heard the door open he must have turned to see if it was me entering. He jumped off his perch and walked toward me, greeting me warmly on such a cold night. I suppose that was a nice start…and finish.

"Jacey? Great to meet you!" he pumped my hand and pecked my cheek.

"Great to meet you, too" I replied with a warm and genuine smile. He seemed nice. I knew right away he was definitely not my type but he did seem nice.

Anyway, as I followed him back to the tiny bar table I mentally noted that I got the dark hair and eyes right, but I think his profile forgot to mention that he was shaped like a bowling pin. *Okay, wine.* I had a glass of that red wine I had been thinking about moments before. Luckily he ordered one too, which I liked because I hate the idea of drinking alone.

After ordering and retrieving our wine glasses at the bar, Contestant #2 jumped back on his bar stool perch and seemed very outgoing and extremely chatty, which is what I had expected from our previous phone conversations. As he continued his balance on the bar stool, he asked me a lot of questions. I don't mind answering questions when the comfort level is right, like when you have some instantaneous connection with someone and *feel* like you *can* share some intimate information because you *want* to. I was under the very quick impression that Contestant #2 liked to share information about himself and, therefore, felt that others must love to equally share. *Not.*

"So, Jacey, what do you do? I am in the marketing business! It's tough because I have to commute to the city everyday and I work a long day." I nodded.

"And you have two girls? I have two girls too! Their names are Blah and Blah. They live with their *mother,* who was nice enough to kick me out last month! Like, where am I supposed to go? Where does she expect me to live? Anyway, I see my girls almost every day. Even though I work long city hours, I still make sure to stop by the house to see them." I nodded some more.

"How long have you been divorced? My divorce isn't even official yet. My ex is giving me such a hard time about *everything!* All she wants is the house and more money, more money, more money! What the fuck, right?" I nodded.

"Do you like the internet dating so far? Because, boy, do I have some stories about that! I basically got right on the internet dating site as soon as I got separated and I've been on some strange dates, I tell ya!" *Gee, wonder why...*

He shared and shared and shared a tremendous amount of information about himself. I think too much. I heard about his wedding, his divorce or separation or whatever he was in the midst of. I heard about his living arrangements, his kids, and previous dating stories. But then, about half way through my glass of wine, I was listening to this contestant rant on about what a bitch his ex-wife was so I started to think he might be a little bitter.

I wasn't quite sure when his sharing looped back around to his ex-wife and I was feeling pretty pissed with myself for not catching it sooner. I was so busy nodding at whatever he was saying, just feeling mildly thankful that I wasn't disclosing as much information as he was. Bottom line, he was still pretty pissed with his ex-wife. I figured I should let him rant on and hopefully get it out of his system. It's not like I was remotely attracted to him and planned on taking him home. I didn't have to pretend to be interested in this business just because I wanted an hour and a half of his time later on. No, I planned to just sit through it, drink my wine, and check my watch every once in a while.

Eventually and thankfully, we were able to get back to us, and I only refer to us as an "us" because it was *us* on the date, nothing more. He was finally either out of breath, out of thoughts, or out of ex-wife rage. He was still completely unattractive to me and even if I was the horniest chick in town, I wasn't going to be sleeping with the bowling pin. To get through the remainder of this meeting, I figured I should lighten up and just be myself. So far, I was being a listener and an answerer, nodding my head up and down like a bobble head as he talked continually about a whole lot of nothing. *Nothing*, like what was in my glass. *More wine, please.*

So I clearly determined there was no attraction on my end, but, I had hung around enough guys in the past to know "how to hang with the boys". I decided to let my guard down just a smidge, interrupt him, and buy the next round. Obviously, for personal reasons, I knew I wasn't getting through another moment of this without a red wine refill, even if I had to buy it myself!

Well, Contestant #2 must have liked the shift in my personality because he got pretty excitable about whatever we ended up talking about, which was still a whole lot of nothing. In fact, he was so excitable (which could have been his wine) that he was insistent upon me giving him *high fives* for every cool or funny thing I said. High fives? Isn't that what you do at sporting events, or a trick you teach a baby, or something you do when you and all your friends are drunk in bar? High fives. Every high five second his hand would rise into the air and wait for me to slap it. Did I mention how small this restaurant was? It was small and the bar was even smaller, although I was sure every diner through the glass partition was watching this guy reach up for a high five. Either they were getting free dinner amusement or maybe they were feeling sorry for me. I wouldn't have felt sorry for me if I were watching, I would have found great amusement at the dumb redhead subjecting herself to this dating debacle. *Everyone get a chuckle at my expense*, I would have! I was wondering if I should have been feeling lucky that all he wanted from me (at the moment) was high fives and not trying to lean in on my personal space or anything.

My second glass of wine was finally finished and probably too quickly for anyone watching. Although, if by some chance someone *was* feeling sorry for me, they would have already presumed I was not an alcoholic, but just slurping it down to get the hell out of there. He offered me another drink but I gracefully declined the third glass, already deciding I was going to have that third glass when I got home....just to reflect, decompress, wallow, whatever.

When the date finally came to an end, I was feeling relieved with a nice little buzz going. Contetstant #2 and I walked out of the restaurant together and happened to have parked in the gas station across the street. He and I started to veer in different directions until we noticed we hadn't said goodbye.

"Well, it was so great meeting you, Jacey, I had a terrific time. Hey, check out my car. Isn't it nice. I betchya my bitch ex-wife wants this from me too"! *Oh jeez. Almost a clean getaway.*

"It was nice to meet you too" I changed the subject.

#2 leaned up toward me because I think I had about 2 inches on him with the boots. He gave me a tight squeeze and another quick cheek peck.

"I'll talk to you soon?" he inquired.

"Yeah, sure, call me."

Later on, over that third glass of red wine, I told some of my single friends about Contestant #2.

"How bad can he be?" they asked.

"Give him another shot, maybe he has some friends", they stated.

"Okay, so he's not your type, but he sounds like he might be fun to be out and about with!" they tried convincing me.

Fine. I'd try again if he called. Maybe I'd be a little lucky and he wouldn't like me enough to call me again. I wasn't that lucky. He called a couple of days later with a free evening. Naively, I had originally told him my free weeknight, probably in the midst of a high five and the need to get some input into the conversation about nothing.

I immediately felt trapped like a mouse in a corner. I *might* have met him out again, strictly for curiosity purposes, had he not become completely insistent upon ordering Chinese food and coming to my house. Coming to my house? Was this guy insane? Since when does TWO glasses of wine allow for visitors?

"I don't really feel comfortable with that", I replied.

"Why?" was his straightforward question. He asked it like a statement, like I was an idiot. There I was, backed in that corner again.

"Because we don't even know each other and I'm not comfortable with strangers in my house, *that's why*", I explained.

I was explaining myself again, just like I did with Contestant #1. *I don't have to explain myself, in fact, I was getting a little pissed.*

#2 says, "Well, nothing has to happen. I can just bring over some Chinese and we can cuddle on the couch".

Ewww, that sealed the deal immediately. If I wasn't a bitch before, I was about to become one now.

"Uh, no. I don't think so and it's a little presumptuous of you to even suggest such an idea. I said I'm not comfortable with it and you should have respected that". For all I know, I could have hung up on him because I never paid any attention to his bowling pin body response. Hey, go strangle yourself with some Lo Mein and high five *that!* Contestant #2 was over.

Notes to self:
No date should ever try to *high five* you.
Presumptuous, Chinese food, visitors *cannot* come over!

Contestant #3

Well, so far, not so good. But I knew I shouldn't give up. I mean, maybe the last couple of guys were not for me and that was okay. I needed to get into the frame of mind that I was *warming up*. I was *warming up* to the idea of going on dates, I was *warming up* to the idea that I was floating out there in cyberspace, and I was *warming up* to the idea that this just might be my reality for a while.

After the high-fiving, Chinese food guy fiasco, I decided to get back up on the horse and ride on. I checked my profile daily-mostly for something to do-and I was getting a lot of hits. People *were* checking me out but often not contacting me. There were two ways a person can contact someone on this thing. First, one could "wink" at someone. This means somebody could send a little wink to let the other person know that they're interested. When the wink was received, one could check the other out and decide whether or not to go further with communication; a reciprocating wink. The other way to contact someone is to just be brave and type something. Well, I was all about being brave (at least, trying to be), so that's the form of communication I chose. I never really typed much, usually just a simple "hi" or "hello". It wasn't much but I was definitely not a *winker*! Winks are weird, and frankly in my eyes, somewhat of a cop-out. If you want to say hi to someone, then just say "hi", you know, open the door a little for someone. I was getting winks and I was getting a few emails, and I mean, *a few*. To be honest, it was kind of discouraging.

Then, Contestant #3 entered the picture. Looking back, I cannot remember many details of this date because only two major things stood out to me that I took along my ride of experience for the laugh when I needed one. This date was from across the river and we decided to meet on my side of the river, which was very nice of him to drive over. That was a courteous start.

I picked out a casual, evening outfit but wasn't feeling all that psyched about meeting him. I *was* getting better at standing in front of my closet, trying to make costume decisions but I really didn't know how to dress to impress when I didn't actually know *who* I was trying to impress. A big, grey area when attempting to primp for a date.

Our phone conversations in the previous days had left a lot to be desired, but I was trying to stay perky and upbeat about the dating world. I kept reminding myself that some things looked better on, than on the hanger. At least that's what my mom had been telling me all my life. Maybe the same was true with dating, too. So I kept trying on, hoping something would suit me.

The meeting was innocent enough. I walked into the joint, which was pretty empty, and met him right away. I hadn't mastered the confidence upon entering into a blind date but I *was* feeling a little better about it. It definitely didn't feel *as* awkward as it had on the last two dates. I guess when you don't know somebody, then you don't know somebody and so what difference does it make anyway? Maybe I *was* getting better at this.

"Hi" I announced, as I approached the bar. "Contestant #3?"

"Yeah, hi. Nice to meet you" he replied as he stood from the barstool to shake my hand.

"Have you been here long" I asked as I noticed his half drunk beer.

"Um, not really, maybe 10 minutes or so." He looked around, "let's go sit over there at one of those empty tables."

He led the way over to the windows that looked out at the Tappan Zee Bridge. He pulled out one of the chairs for me and I draped my purse on the chair corner and quietly sat down. I wish I had grabbed a beer before sitting because now he had something to sip on and I didn't. Thankfully the bartender came from around her safe haven and took my drink order.

"I'll just have a Coors Light, please" I said.

She smiled "sure", and walked off. I wondered if #3 wanted to order another for himself because if so, she didn't give him the time of day to do that. Oh well.

As I took in the whole package of Contestant #3, I noticed that he was very tall, lanky, and somewhat hunched at the neckline. I'm pretty sure his profile stated that he was tall, athletic, and toned. Not that it makes a difference, really, but it just didn't seem very accurate to me. The other piece of this evening that was definitely inaccurate was the fact that somewhere between posting his photo and meeting me, he had lost pretty much all of his hair. There were some stray strands, neatly plopped on his head, but for the most part (of his head), he was bald. His photos really didn't portray that aspect of him at all. Again, not that it makes a big difference what a person looks like or the amount of hair he had (or didn't). It was his misperception of himself that worried me a little. This guy turned out to look exactly opposite of what he entered in his profile. My flags went up. *Red flag, red flag!*

We sat in a fairly empty restaurant bar during on off-season on the river. The view was still pretty enough to gaze at with the bridge in the background all lit up. Thank goodness for the bridge, because it was a much better view than what was sitting across from me. Just my personal taste, that's all. We had a couple of beers and chitchatted about basic stuff but I found myself struggling to fill the awkward silences that kept invading the space between us.

"So you're from Rockland" I stated, already knowing this from one of our bland phone chats. I was hoping he would roll with it and make more than one sentence at a time.

"Yup" he replied.

I nodded. So this was how it was going to go.

"They have great street fairs in Nyack, I have been to a bunch of them over the years" I added, leaving the door *wide* open for a multiple sentence reply.

"I have heard about those. Never been, though"

A whole two sentences. Fragmented sentences.

I nodded again and gazed out the window. I believed I was reaching a dating growth spurt deep within my head and I eventually saw no real reason in prolonging the agony of this meeting. I wasn't planning on another beer so I mildly mentioned to him that I had other plans to get to.

"Well, I think I should probably hit the road" I said

"You don't want another drink?"

"No, because I have to drive."

"Well, we don't have to drink anymore, we could just sit and talk for a while longer."

The very thought of this was sounding about as good as chewing my beer bottle to pieces.

"I actually have to meet up with some friends in about 20 minutes" I informed.

He seemed a little surprised with this statement and his thinning eyebrows wrinkled into his shiny head.

"Well, I figured we would just meet for drinks to meet and see each other" I continued, seeing now that I might have been hurting his feelings.

There I was, explaining myself again for the third time since I paid up for a screen name. I was starting to wonder if he was feeling some match made in heaven but I stood my ground about having to meet up with friends (which I was).

"I hope I didn't cut into your night too much, I know it's still kind of early…" I politely added, trying to take away the apparent sting on his face.

"No, no it's fine. It's a beautiful night and I can go meet up with one of my friends too," #3 replied.

"Oh, that's good", I said, and continued, "What do you have planned for the rest of the night?"

"Well, since it's such a clear night, I'll probably call my friend and we'll just lie on the grass and look up at the stars."

Huh?

"Look at the stars?" I asked, with twisted confusion.

"Yeah, I'm really into astronomy. Maybe on our next date we can look at the stars together." He raised his eyebrows up and down at me.

I had a feeling this guys head was *stuck up* in the stars!

"Uh, yeah, sure, I like stars." And I do, with the right person, like my astrologist, who comes over for parties and gives me my readings over a few glasses of wine. I love *her* stars!

Well, it was at that moment that I decided this date would not suit me and it wasn't even that great on the hanger either. I started fidgeting my exit, knowing that I was putting Contestant #3 back on the rack for someone else to rifle through. I knocked back the rest of my beer and gently took hold of my purse hanging from my chair.

Thankfully, he took the hint gracefully and got up to walk out with me. My final, parting thoughts while leaving the restaurant, *basically, this guy was a little bit of a geek, probably without a mirror in his house to see what he actually looks like.*

He walked me out to my car like a gentleman, which, luckily, was parked right in front with light upon it. I wasn't very thrilled with a stranger walking me to my car on a quiet night.

"I had a really nice time with you tonight" he said as he looked down to me.

"Yes, it was nice" I replied, eyeing my car door already.

"Well, I'm looking forward to our stargazing evening on our next date" he added.

"Yes, that would be great" I blatantly lied, *without guilt.* I knew that date would never happen. *Ever.*

I thanked him for the drinks and politely intended to give him a quick peck on the cheek. I really have no problem with that, and anybody that knows the meaning of a peck knows it's *just* a polite thing. Not him. The lanky, bald guy with stray floating hairs in the breeze turned on me in the last, split second and landed his skinny little lips on my polite, cheek peck. *Ewwww!* I left.

In the car I reflected on that last hour of my life while on my way to meet my friends. Stargazer-sneaky kisser were the two things I would never forget. Contestant #3 was over!

Notes to self:
Some people may not actually *own* a mirror at home.
Geeky dates *will* try sneaky kisses!

A Break-Take 1

I needed a break. I figured since I never really wanted to do this online thing in the first place, I deserved a break from this kind of dating trauma! I stopped my online membership after three months or so and removed my well thought out profile from public viewing so that I could try to get a handle on the actual prospects for me in this single, dating world. I felt like I signed up mostly for my mother and definitely for the curious experience and I got a pretty good taste of it in three months. *Was I ready? I doubt it. Was my heart into it? I doubt it. Was I giving guys a fair chance? I doubt that, too.* Time for a break.

Just because I signed off did not mean I had guys banging down my door and great dates lined up. I didn't. In fact, I fell into a deeper slump trying to figure out where a thirty year old single mother belonged, while making a life for two kids in the suburbs. I was really stumped. My mother continued to bring me clippings from the newspaper about single gatherings, new dating websites, and support groups for divorcees. Although I knew she was quietly worried about me and trying to help, she was actually starting to drive me crazy. Every so often another clipping would be strategically placed somewhere in my house that I would come upon by chance. I knew it wasn't me because I didn't read the paper so these little articles were mysteriously sneaking into my house and sounding their silent siren at me, *read me, read me!* I usually made a passing glance through the article just so I could withstand the possible pop quiz my mother gave me when I heard her say;

"Did you see the article that was on the living room buffet?"

"Did you happen to notice the clipping on your kitchen table?"

"Did you read it? What do you think? Is it something you might want to tryyyyy?" *No!*

The summer arrived, which I always looked forward to except that my mind blocks out the part that my friends travel all over the place throughout the summer! My kids were too young for camp, I wasn't working, and it was Africa hot to get motivated to do anything. So I sat. I sat and I sat and I cried and I sat some more. My mother was worried and stopped acting like the Newspaper Clipping Fairy for the time being. She began suggesting online stuff again or even therapy. How one relates to another, I'm not sure, but I think she was grasping at any idea to help me get my feet on the ground.

I was officially depressed, because what person sits around the house all day in their pajamas on beautiful, sunny, summer days? I was overwhelmed with the divorce proceedings, single-parenting, finances, and sadness. I really felt like no online service or therapy session was going to fix me at that moment. *Really, what guy (or therapist, for that matter) would really want to take that on anyway?* What was worse was that I had two little girls that desperately needed my attention and some fresh air and I couldn't get any more motivated than to put on Sesame Street for them. How pathetic.

On another wonderfully, bright day in my pajamas, my dark brain cloud finally lightened up when my friend called.

"Come into the city tonight!" she demanded.

"There are a bunch of rugby players here from Scotland and it should be a really fun time!"

"Yeah?" I replied with a handful of hesitation.

I wasn't sure I was feeling up for the task. The idea of moving my body from the couch that stored the imprint of my ass, taking a shower for more purpose than not to just smell, and arranging kid coverage that was longer than a quick stint to the store was almost too much for me to think about at once. It would've been so much easier if she called, saying she'd be over to pick me up in an hour, and left it at that. *Lighten up*, I screamed into my brain cloud! Holy crap, I was annoying myself with all the damn self-pity.

"What's the plan?" I asked.

She gave me the plan of nothing special, just to come into the city, meet her, meet them and rambled off the address to me. *Okay. I'll go*, I thought. That little nagging voice deep within me (my cricket) knew that I needed to get out of the house, get with people, and maybe have a few laughs.

My cricket voice was able to beat the crap out of my dark brain cloud and I was really getting sick of succumbing to martyrdom, so I jumped in the shower, put on a new face, dressed in the almighty, slimming black outfit, and hopped on a train. Getting off my ass, scrubbing my body, and dropping the kids off wasn't as bad as I expected it to be.

I met my friend in the sweltering city heat but the temperature was put into perspective for me when I watched a dozen Scottish men climb out of cabs in wool kilts. Apparently, Scottish evening attire doesn't coincide with the weather of August in New York and probably going commando doesn't help their under-the-wool situation. Yes, they go commando.

I grabbed my first giggle of the night when I watched these six foot five men climbing out of a yellow taxi like clowns falling out of those miniature cars at a circus. They just kept coming and I had no idea how they all fit in there in the first place! One rugby player after another slowly made their way out of the tiny cabs and they would then stretch to their full height, averaging at about 6 foot 5. *Wow.*

The night was actually quite fun, although I couldn't understand a single word anyone was saying. Their accent was strong and rich and I found that the more I drank, the better I understood! So I drank. I drank and I laughed and I drank and I even flirted until.....I was kissed. Wow, was I kissed. Way downtown in the midst of a crowded, yet seedy bar, I was balancing on a beat up wooden stool chatting it up with whomever I understood at that very moment. I had had my eye on this particular stranger all evening but we had never really gotten around to talking.

This gorgeous, Scottish man in a hot, woolen kilt slowly approached me with a look of pure determination in his eyes. He knew what he was about to do and something told me that I knew it too. He stood before me, looking down upon me and my tiny barstool and laid one right on my lips. It was as though he had been planning that moment of perfection all evening, so I just went with it and enjoyed the lip lock. I almost fell off my bar stool with surprise but I saved myself, realized what was happening, and adapted like a champ! It had been a while but thank goodness I still knew how to kiss! In fact, so did he and there is really nothing better than two people who really know how to kiss! It was exactly the thing I needed, considering I was rotting on my living room sofa just hours ago.

After that special little moment, the night sped by at record speed and it was time to catch my train home. I didn't want to leave the fun party but I didn't want to over do it on my first night apart from my big, dark, brain cloud. I might've gone into shock, unable to adapt and transition from depressive to happy, all within a few hours.

It was a really fun night and I got out of the house for the evening. It turned my spirit up a little the following day until I received another call from my hostess friend.

"He wants to see you again. Get dressed. Get coverage. We have plans" she barked.

"Jesus! Does he even remember me?" I asked.

"Are you *kidding?* He hasn't stopped talking about you and half the things he says I can barely understand!" she cackled.

"Oh my God. Well, what are we doing?"

"Rugby game in Connecticut. I'll pick you up in a little while. Can you get coverage for the girls?"

"Um, let me work on that. I'll call you back in a few minutes."

"Really try because he seriously has *not* stopped asking about you!" she laughed again. "What did you *do* to him?" she laughed some more.

"Nothing! He walked up to me, kissed me like a rock star, and then I caught my train! I'll call you in a few".

I was able to get some sleepover coverage from my ex who happened to be speaking to me at the time. He was living locally and apparently didn't have a girlfriend taking up all his time so he was happy to help. Those were the days.

My friend picked me up as planned and we drove off to a rugby game in Connecticut, trying to reminisce about the evening before and why this guy might be so interested. We laughed about our new friends, while listening to music and smoking cigarettes. I was getting a little excited and I knew *nothing* about rugby!

I spent most of the week with the rugby team and my new kissing friend from Scotland. I spent the week traveling from New York to the border of Connecticut to watch rugby games that I knew nothing of, party in bars at the 'drink up', and flirt with the out-of-towners. I finagled and wrangled every possible baby-sitting coverage that I could, just so I could enjoy myself for the first time in a *long* time. Interesting how just a few days before, I couldn't bear the idea of exerting the energy into finding baby-sitting coverage!

The hot, kilted man turned out to be a perfect gentleman, a fabulous rugby player, and, *very* married. Unfortunately, we passed the point of kissing and we decided to take it that final step further- *my house*. I was worried and nervous because I hadn't brought anyone home to my house before, my bed before, my world before. I hadn't been feeling very sexy or attractive up until this particular week, yet I wasn't too thrilled about taking off any article of clothing for anyone to see either. I was feeling extremely nervous about the prospect of bringing home a man that I knew belonged to someone else so I needed to confer with my 'people' first.

The day of our planned evening, I made a couple of phone calls to my best friends, Thelma and Louise. Those phone calls sparked other phone calls and I was visually picturing a T.V. screen with 12 separate blocks of people with phones to their ears, spreading news to each other about what I was about to embark on. The bottom line: my friends knew how unhappy I had been the last few months and how happy I'd been in the past few days.

"Puh-lease, he's from *another country* for God sake, you'll never see him again."

"Well, if you think you can handle it, *go for it.*"

"*Wait a minute*, who's this guy and where's he from?"

"Absolutely have fun, but whatever you do, *don't* give him your number!"

I was so surprised with what my friends were saying that I felt this overwhelming confidence and support to just do what I wanted for the first time in a *really* long time. I met him later on, had a great night, and brought him home with me.

He was completely in awe of my home, nicknaming it the "White House", stating that no one in Scotland had houses of this size. My house was very average, considering where I lived so I wasn't really seeing the big deal. He walked around a bit and I gave him a completely unnecessary grand tour. He admired all of the photos around the house and commented on the beauty of my little girls. *I was such a sucker.*

Eventually we made it upstairs to my bedroom and things kicked in pretty gracefully. I felt weirdly comfortable with him but still felt strange having someone in my bed other than my husband, ex-husband. I tried to imagine us in a place other than *my* bed and that helped me feel a little less inhibited. I thought of the peaceful, romantic sound of the ocean. I pretended we were on an island far from our homes with the waves quietly breaking in the background and the warm breeze blowing through the picture windows, as the sheer curtains waved and danced in the moonlight. We didn't need music, for our partnered breathing was all the rhythm we needed. We didn't need words because the look from one pair of seductive eyes to another was all we needed to communicate our needs and wants. We didn't need anything other than our bodies meshing in sync to the beating of our pounding hearts as we were pressed skin to skin. In my head, we moved to the ebb and flow of the crashing waves below the open window. In my ears, I listened to the man whispering his desires with hot breath, blowing in and out like the breeze through the curtains. In my hands, I felt the softness of his skin as I ran my fingertips along the width of his muscular back. I was completely lost in the moment, not realizing where I was anymore, the beach or my own bed.

He was gentle, and sensitive, and totally unselfish as we consummated this unexpected and strangely intimate relationship that only lasted a week. We had a truly, beautiful night and it was so nice to finally fall asleep in someone's arms again. He had large, rugby arms that my head nestled into perfectly. It had been a long, long time since I was able to nestle into anyone and the comfort and security I felt was very peaceful for me.

The next morning, the comfortable, peaceful, secure feeling diminished as I was dreading the idea of getting out of bed with no clothes on. Secretly, I was hoping he would have to pee or something and get up first so I could quickly slip on a tee-shirt and sweats. I guess he was more of a lounger, sprawled out in bed, stretching and cuddling. Well, I couldn't take it any longer and I was going to pee myself if no one made a move. I started to fidget quite a bit and I think he knew something was up. I knew that I was going to have to succumb to early morning daylight and the sighting of my ass that I wasn't proud of at the moment. Well, *ever*.

So, the beauty of a few hours ago was over. The safeness of the moonlit darkness was gone. The sound of waves meeting the shore was replaced by the faint sound of the garbage truck down the street and, of course, my thoughts immediately wondered how to gracefully run downstairs and get the cans to the curb! My senses were smacking my reality around and mocking the extreme difference of just a few simple hours ago. Rather than my heart beating so hard for the sensual romance, it was now beating so hard for so many ridiculous reasons, like daylight, possible humiliation, cellulite, and the garbage cans!

I slowly made a move to sit up and wriggle my way to the edge of the bed. I quickly glanced around the surrounding floor, hoping there would be some article of clothing for me to snatch up with my toes and escape into. No. No clothing lying about on my side of the bed. *It figured.*

I decided that this was a one shot deal and I would never see him again anyway. The deed had already been done and it was extremely enjoyable for both of us, so really, what's a glimpse of my fat ass anyway??? I stood up and moved the three feet across the floor to grab a pair of pajama bottoms off the wicker trunk at the end of my bed. I didn't care about being topless, for those girls are my better assets, my *ass* was not! Nevertheless, the fact that my caboose was now covered up made me feel a little more comfortable with daylight streaming in.

It seemed I worried for nothing because this wonderful man told me how beautiful I looked in the morning, how beautiful he thought my body was, and how he wanted to take a shower with me. *Whoa!* I think I had to draw the line with the shower because that would require full frontal and backside nudity that I definitely wasn't ready for, although it probably would have done endless, long-term wonders for my struggling self-esteem. In retrospect, I wish I *had* taken that shower but there's no point in the shoulda, woulda, coulda. He took a shower and I found clothes to throw on in the meantime.

By the end of the week and at the time of his departure back to his homeland of Inverness, he claimed his undying love for me in a parking lot and he even bought me a pretty bracelet to remember him by. Along with the bracelet, he left behind his rugby jersey, which was drenched of his body scent.

When it was time to bid farewell, it was a very emotional and tearful encounter, mostly for me. I believe he was sad because this was unexpected for him, as well. But, I did most of the crying because I was feeling somewhat attached and maybe mildly clingy, considering how lonely I had been just a week before. He told me he fell in love with me with a hint of embarrassment in his voice, and he held me for what seemed like hours. Not very romantic in the parking lot of the Super 8 Motel that he was staying in, but locations were limited since the rest of his country was hooting and hollering from the upstairs windows!

Anyway, how does this happen in a week? I'm sure I don't know. But, I've heard stories like this all my life and never thought it would happen to me. *Clearly, it can!*

As we parted ways, he returned to ask me *one* more thing. I dreaded this because all I heard in my head was my girlfriend's voice saying, 'whatever you do, *do not* give him your number'. She said 'let it be what it is and say goodbye'. Lastly, she added 'promise me you won't give him your number!' I promised, I promised, and I promised. Then, in a split second, I broke my promise. *Sorry.*

So the Scotsman and I kept in touch for *six* long months. I was talking to him everyday during my lunchtime and his closing time (5 hour time difference). He remained so sweet and really became my friend. I was able to vent to him about all the emotional divorce stuff and he supported me fully, with always the right thing to say. I may have really loved him but the truth was, I was having an affair with my AT&T calling card and that was pathetic. He shared with me his unhappiness at home which somewhat justified our keeping in touch but he remained married and that wasn't going to change. *Even if it had changed, did I really think he would up and move to New York?* Not really, but my little fantasy was pleasant enough for me.

I became a pro with the calling card, with my cell phone and.... with....text messaging. What fun that was! It was so much fun that the two of us became quite daring with our text messages, not really paying much attention to the reality of the situation.

About six months to the day of our meeting I received a text from him that made my stomach somersault.

"She red ur tx 2 me. Spk 2mrw".

Uh oh. Okay, so his wife had read my text and thankfully, it was a message that had absolutely no innuendos whatsoever. Shocking, considering all the others had. Maybe that was a sign. A sign from who?

I didn't know but it was a sign from somebody saying *"Stop this shit, he isn't yours!"* I think that was the little voice in my head, like that Jiminy Cricket guy, the conscience! I definitely have a cricket in my head but sometimes he has to really scream in there or slap me around a little. I heard him this time.

So I faced the inevitable the next day and ended it sadly with my Scottish kilt man. It deeply saddened me because I really felt more than I had ever expected to with him. I wanted to be with him, I wanted him pack his stuff and move here, I wanted him to find happiness with me, too. However, I did not want him to ever leave his child and I knew he would resent me eternally if I had ever suggested such an idea. Perhaps it was never meant to be, but deep down, I know fate stepped in for me and there was a reason behind this relationship. This situation really left me a little heart broken. I guess a "break" is really a break after all.

Notes to self:
Someone available *and* in the same country helps.
Calling cards make lousy lovers.

A Break- Take 2

After a few tearful and sobbish moments I was able to bounce back a little. I figured out that although maybe it wasn't meant to be with my Scottish man, maybe he was meant to be in my life, even for just that short while. I will always see him as my angel. He was a beautiful man that floated into my life at one of my darkest moments. Moments when I felt utterly rejected and discarded. Moments when I felt ugly and fat. Moments of deep despair, loneliness, and sadness.

Just like an angel, he drifted to me from wherever the European and American clouds connected and told me I was beautiful, making me feel as though I was as beautiful as his words. He looked into my eyes when he talked to me and he treated me like a woman with a perfect mix of sexuality and feminism. He was the angel of my ego. He saved my ego and everything I had begun thinking about myself. He showed me that I was a woman who was worthy of love, care and respect. He was the first man I had been with since my ex-husband had left me. He would remain truly unforgettable forever.

I guess my friends noticed some subtle, and I mean *subtle*, changes in my confidence. Although I was coping with a bit of unexpected sadness, I was holding my head a little higher and actually willing to get through my days outside of the house and dressed in something other than pajamas. Maybe…I was beginning to grow.

However, after witnessing many of my spontaneous crying outbursts, they decided it was time to set me up. It wasn't like I was having a full thrown tantrum of tears, it just seemed as though every time I spoke of Scotland, I became tearful and weepy all over again. I was still wallowing because it was unfair. *Poor me* because it was unfair for me to steal somebody else's man. *Poor me* because he lived too far away to conduct a proper affair. *Poor me* because I needed him back. Oh, *poor me*.

Like my friends, I also decided that maybe it was time to be set up, too. Sometimes I had to wonder if I was being set up for the sake of two people getting together or if I was being set up for disaster. Not that my friends would purposely set me up for disaster, so maybe "set-up" should take on a new catch phrase like "get together", or "meet and greet" or anything besides being "set-up". Athletic plays are set up. Crime stings are set up. "Set up" can also refer to being framed in a situation that you shouldn't be in or were never a part of in the first place! I was being set up.

On a day with no purpose or meaning at all, I met my best friend, Louise, for lunch while she was escaping from work on a well-deserved lunch break. We met up the street from my house at a local pizza place and huddled into one of the booths with two huge slices of loaded up pizza. We were deep in conversation over the Scottish man and I was sharing some words of wisdom passed on by my mother. My mother continued to remain concerned for my well-being while continuing to stew over her blatant hatred for my ex-husband. She figured any of my unhappiness, whether brought on by my own poor choices or brought on by somebody else's poor choices, was all directly related to what an asshole she thought he was to me.

"We need to find you a nice, single father who understands your life", she would say to me.

"You, know, someone who understands kids, visitation, and who doesn't care that you have an asshole for an ex-husband". Or, according to my new name for him; *exhole.*

"I know, I know", I would reply, for the lack of anything else to respond with.

The truth was, I didn't know who to be set up with, or what kind of man would understand me. I had no idea who could set me up since half my friends were just recently married in the first place! What was I supposed to do? Get my phone book out and start calling everyone I know?

Hey, it's me. Have anyone to set me up with?

Hi. Me again. Know any single fathers who might understand me?

What's up? Do you happen to have a single brother that I never knew about?

Bingo!!! Over those slices of loaded pizzas, discussing my absent love life, and my mother's concerns for me, Louise heard my words "I think I'm ready". She jumped on it while trying to swallow a big glob of cheesy pizza. While she was chewing and swallowing, she used the moment to ponder her thoughts. I actually thought I saw a light bulb shining over her highlighted blond hair. She finished chewing her bite of pizza, and raised her eyebrows.

The next words floored me but the greatest part was that she gave me a choice; her brother (whom my friends and I have been lusting over for 15 years) or, her husbands close friend (whom, oddly enough, I had never met before). I was so excited, yet relieved, that she actually *had* someone to set me up with because it didn't make me seem like such a lost cause after all. *And*, it would make my mother so happy for the time being. So, regarding the former lustful fantasies of her brother, I decided to try the "set-up" with him over the newly separated friend of her husband.

The set-up was easy because we knew each other. We weren't close by any means and it had been a while since I had seen him. A lot had changed over the many years for both of us and we didn't live close enough to move within the same, or even similar social circle. He had a small son and was in the midst of doing the single dad thing. He and his son were spending a lot of time around Louise's house with her kids so all the cousins could hang out. I wasn't sure if he would really go for the idea of being set up with me. I mean, I *was* one of her pesky friends many years ago that would giggle like an idiot when he was nearby. For the record…I wasn't the *only* giggling idiot, though.

He seemed game at her suggestion of linking the two of us together and I supposed it was now or never, so I was game too. It quickly took on a little life of its own, as we found ourselves hanging out at her safe house and allowing all the kids to play together. Throwing food on the grill became second nature and relaxing, watching t.v. on the couch became comfortable. Days turned into evenings on lazy Sundays and playful banter mixed with solid conversation kept the ball rolling. I was feeling kind of happy about this.

Eventually, it was time to graduate to a kidless evening, so Louise arranged a triple date to have a nice dinner at a restaurant. It was fun. *Really*. I was a total nervous wreck, but it was fun. *Really*. I really liked him with kids and without. I guess I just really liked him. He was easy to talk to, laugh with, and the chemistry between us was a bonus too!

On the night of our date , I picked out a semi-chic outfit, all black of course, and made myself feel as pretty as I could, trying to ignore the intense butterflies in my belly that were doing their best to make me puke. We met at Louise's safe house and all rode along together to meet the other couple at the restaurant.

We started with drinks in the bar, which was much needed to loosen the mood for me. Then, eventually, we sat at a large, round table in the back corner of the restaurant. The dinner was fabulous with a fun group of people, laughing and storytelling throughout the evening. There was no stress, pressure or nerves getting the best of me and it ended up being quite comfortable as he picked off my plate with ease, as though we had been eating together for years.

Over the next few months, we had some dinners out in his local town, continued to hang out with the kids, went to a concert together in Manhattan, and I even took him to a friends wedding. Getting him to go to the wedding with me was torture in itself, as I needed a whole new set of balls to ask him to come. I didn't know how to ask a guy to a wedding or to anywhere!

"So, I don't know if you've heard from Louise, but our friend Bobby is getting married…."

"Yeah, she mentioned that the other day" he replied.

This wasn't going to be easy.

"Well, I was invited to bring a date" I said cautiously.

"You were…"

Torture.

"Yeah. So do you think maybe you'd wanna come with me? It should be fun and we would be with Louise and Patrick and a whole bunch of other people" I said.

"I think it should be fine. I have to see if I have visitation that day because I would need my mom to cover" he stated.

"Can I let you know?" he added.

Oh my God. Not even a straight answer.

"Yeah sure, but don't forget because I have to send the response card in, like yesterday" I said.

"No problem, I'll find out but, yeah, I wanna go".

Thank God.

He forgot to check on that little detail in days to come and Louise had to finalize my wedding date plans. It was slightly embarrassing within an already personally awkward moment for myself. Another learning experience. Another growth spurt.

As it turned out, it wasn't that hard after all and once he showed up in my driveway and I was wearing a pretty dress, I felt really ready to take it on. I wouldn't want to do it again, though.

All a good time. All with good conversation. All with many laughs. All with fabulous chemistry. I really did like him and I was over the childhood, lustful fantasies because now he was a real man before my eyes. All those times in past years when I figured he saw me as a pain in the ass friend of his sisters was all just a memory at this point. We were real adults, on real dates, having real lustful sex!

I was slowly getting over the sexual confidence problem I may have experienced with Commando Kilt Man. In this relationship, I was definitely getting more practice with the good ole' romp and things certainly had a bit of a different feel, which might have left an occasional passion mark, or two. I wasn't feeling as emotionally connected with body and mind, rather just body on body and boy, did he do a body good….my body! It was tough to kiss and tell with Louise about this one because having sex with her brother really fell into that "TMI" category of a friendship. Up until this point in my life, I never thought best friends could have a "TMI" category, but I suppose poor Louise trying to wrap her head around her best friend and her brother hitting it in every other room was probably Too Much Information for her to process, or care to process, for that matter! I just let her think what she wanted to because we both knew what was going on. Besides, the post-laid, perma-smile plastered on my face would have been a dead give away anyway!

So even though the time was fun, believe me, when I say that nothing is perfect, even with a great guy and great sex. There was, on occasion, the strangeness of dates with him too. Like, for instance, the political date. I named it the political date after I watched my best friend's husband and my best friend's brother get into a huge verbal argument and physical escalade over the next presidential election. Now, this was before Obama's time, but apparently just as controversial! My friend, Louise, being quite pregnant at the time, decided to cut her evening a little shorter than the three of us. She went home for a decent night sleep which, in retrospect, is probably what I should have done, too. In any case, the verbal argument over both presidential candidates quickly turned into barstool-flipping words and the heave-ho out the door. *Did I know how to drive back to the house? No. Did we even have a car to drive back in? No.* But, apparently being a Republican or a Democrat was taking precedence over our ride home.

After I was able to interrupt the two screaming men for a moment, in between them catching their breaths for the next debate, one of them was able to call us a cab. We waited in the chilly spring night for a cab to come to our, I mean *my*, rescue. I was able to separate them in the car like a mother of two teenaged boys. One in the front, one in the back. However, they proceeded to violently argue over the back of the front seat the entire way home. Well, almost the whole way home. Actually, I had no idea where we were so we might have been close to home or not. The yelling became so loud, that the cabbie felt the need to pull over and make them finish this on the side of the road. However, the cabbie had no intention on hanging around to see who the winner was. *Do I stay and watch or do I get in the cab and go?* As I was making my fleeting decision to get in the cab, the guys finished their argument alright, swinging and attacking each other right over the guard rail! It was at that defining moment, after they disappeared down the hill, when I decided to get in and tell the cabbie to just go. Let him figure out how to get me home *without* the other two boneheads! Besides, they were already tumbling down the other side of the guard rail anyway. *Great date.*

The cab pulled into the driveway, where the house looked so calm and peaceful. I got out, paid him, and asked him to drive back the way we came to see if the boys had appeared back over the guard rail yet. He agreed and off he went. I decided to unwind from this disaster with a cigarette outside by my car. As I took a few leisurely and relaxing drags, I saw the shadows of approaching headlights behind me. For a split second I had wondered if that was the cab again and then my suspicions were confirmed when I overheard more yelling and screaming coming from inside the cab. I guess the cabdriver found the guys.

Maybe this should have helped me foresee the future, or at least make me feel more confident about my present dating situation. It didn't, really. Looking back, this particular date was as disastrous as some of the blind dates on the website so far! However, I really *did* like him so I decided that I would attempt the good with the bad, the cuddle to the yell, the dinner to the guard rail, all - for the time being.

As comfortable as I felt around this guy, I still couldn't shake the nerves he conjured up in me. I had tremendous difficulty calling him, although I know it comes as second nature in this day and age for a woman to call a man. If one wasn't calling, they were easily texting, IMing, or emailing, none of which makes me feel any more comfortable. I guess I was still really old school. I just couldn't get that number dialed without the sudden urge to puke my guts out all over the kitchen floor. It was a simple thing to do. Pick up the phone, press the numbers, listen to the ring, and say hello. *Puke!*

Instead of burdening Louise with this nauseous issue I had, I would call my other best friend, Thelma, tell her what my problem was, and then, like a child in trouble, she would literally count to three for me. What did this mean? Well, she would pep me up, motivate me, get me going, whatever you want to call it. Then, when she hit the number three she would hang up on me. At that point, I was to hang up with her too and immediately dial his number before I lost my nerve and puke on the kitchen floor. To conclude this ridiculous, middle school ritual, I would have to call Thelma back and relay whatever I just said to him or his voicemail, whichever one I got! *Hello? Balls anyone?* Because clearly I had none!

Perhaps, it was his apparent obliviousness about me. Perhaps, it was his busy schedule. Perhaps, it was my own idiotic mentality telling myself that I wasn't quite good enough. Perhaps it was just his aloof actions in general, like when I was waiting on pins and needles for his response to take me to the wedding. His sister adamantly responded on his behalf that he was coming, but a confirming phone call from him really would have sealed the deal for me. That day of the wedding, I went about my usual routine of getting fancy for an event of that kind, with constant worries popping through that he wasn't going to be exiting their car when they all came to pick me up! *Who needed that?*

Aloofness. Something I would have to try to master somewhere in my lifetime because it seems to have a magical power on the opposite person! The wonderful thing about being aloof was that it never made him a bad guy, or an insensitive guy. It made him aloof, somewhat spacey, pretty non-committal, just a *whatever* kind of attitude. Are people born with that genetic quality or is it learned over time? I wanted some.

On top of everything, I was actually losing sleep over him. Why? I have no idea. Maybe I wasn't feeling my aloof yet. My nerves and emotions had really gotten the best of me. Looking back, I'm sure I was completely twisted up over the first potential idea of a dating relationship. Dating a person. Not *a* date with a person, but *dates* with a person. The *same* person. Frightening. For most of that relationship I second guessed myself into oblivion. I couldn't understand why this guy was attracted to me, why he wanted to date me, and when was he going to wake up and change his mind about me. After all those lustful fantasies in my early twenties about him, I was now living them and I couldn't figure out how or why. I wasn't quite up there in the self-esteem extreme yet and the only ounce of confidence I had to go on had already left the country during my last "break".

So there I was, dating my best friend's incredibly hot brother, making phone calls on the count of three, and losing sleep to boot! I tried to just go with it, and it was going....fine.

But...then one day, he never called back. Just didn't. I left a couple of messages with the bile rising up through my insides every time, but I'm no a fool and I have a good amount of pride, so I didn't harass him with any more calls. Instead, I just kind of wondered what the hell happened. Of course everyone has baggage, we wouldn't be very human if we didn't. I knew he had been dealing with a lot from his ex recently and he had even taken time out to share some of those details with me in the last few months. Of course we all have busy schedules between work and kids and I already knew he had been trying to make a successful go of his business while trying to juggle whatever child visitation his ex gifted him with at her convenience. Of course we all second guess ourselves in a blooming situation. Maybe he was, maybe he wasn't. I was. Maybe.... he was just beyond aloof.

Poor Louise found herself stuck in the middle of a touchy situation and actually was feeling a little pissed off with her brother. I appreciated that, but I felt bad about it, too. It really got me down for the remainder of the summer because I wondered *"why"* all the time. *Why not even a phone call back? Why not a smidgen of honesty? Why am I not good enough? Why do I have to endure more heartbreak?* Well, maybe not heartbreak, but definitely a little ache. And, why did I find myself with big, ugly, purple, sleep-deprived bags under my eyes? Its one thing to feel like shit on the inside, but one should consider drawing a personal line when looking like shit on the outside. I had enough baggage to worry about without having to walk around with more bags under my eyes.

Finally, I made a spontaneous decision to leave one final message on his voice mail that I had developed more of a relationship with. For this particular phone call, I didn't *need* the count of three to dial. I expressed my low level of disappointment and I told him I had expected a little more honesty from him. I wished him a nice life. I hung up. I didn't feel better, but I was hoping that the idea of having the last word would eventually lighten my spirit a little. I was hoping to help give myself a little closure on a situation that seemed to be heading in an upbeat direction. I think I actually managed that for myself. I actually did feel better by giving myself the opportunity to have the last word.

I think it was good for everybody all around and a lesson was definitely learned from this....maybe we shouldn't set up family and friends. Obviously if it were to happen on its own, nobody can really control that, but searching it out purposefully might be setting ourselves up for disaster. And that was the first "set-up".

Notes to self:
Don't rely on former lusts for a successful "set-up"!
The last word *definitely* helps you feel a *little* better!

A Break- Take 3

After a number of weeks, I was feeling pretty okay about my final phone call. I wasn't bitchy or mean, just honest, which is what I expected in return in the first place. So I went about my life and finished out the summer somewhat peacefully. I spent time on the beach with my girls until sunset. I spent time with my girlfriends, talking and laughing like no other crew could ever attempt to do as good as us. I spent time preparing for my first big-girl job as a teacher's assistant in the reading department of a local school. I was definitely filling my time but, unfortunately, I was no better in the love life department than before.

On a fairly balmy evening very late in August, Louise and I sat outside on her front porch sipping wine and smoking cigarettes talking about anything and everything. Very little about her brother was mentioned, but I think we both knew not to get into it too much. There was no doubt that we both had the same feelings about how it unfolded, so there was really no need to put it into actual words and kill our wine buzz. We sat out there for a long time, chitchatting away the evening, staring at the stars during comfortable lulls as only close friends can share, when she finally brought up the "other" guy. *Buzz kill or butterflies?*

"The one who just got separated?" I asked.

"Yeah, but I think he might be ready to meet you", she replied. "Besides, he's been separated for like a year now", she added.

"Yeah?" I inquired.

"Yeah, and he's *really* nice. He's a good dad, *and* he has a smokin' body!"

Well, if I put those three things together, what's not to like about being set-up…again. Sounds like I'd be hitting the trifecta, doesn't it? *Ha!* Even though he sounded too good to be true, I wasn't too keen on the idea of being set-up again and, so far, my track record during my 'break' from online dating was 0 for 2.

Hesitating, I replied, "Fine. But do it fast before I change my mind."

'Fast' was an understatement. When I was at her house the following weekend, in walked the guy, clearly coming from the gym. He was just "stopping by" to have a couple of beers with Louise's husband. I met him, probably because that's what I was *supposed* to do. He had a nice, strong handshake, a really attractive face, and…. a smokin' body! He also seemed *really* nice. One can't be too careful of *really* nice, but I'll get back to that later.

So, with the onset of fall in the air, fall would be the key word for this guy. I was definitely falling faster than the leaves off the trees in autumn! We met a few more times at my friend's house with spontaneous pop over visits, until one evening, after we all had plenty of cocktails, he was nice enough to spread a blanket down on the floor so I wouldn't get harsh rug burn on my lower back! I wasn't sure if it was the one-too-many-cocktails or the fact that I was having a little dry spell in the sexual content area of my life or that maybe he was so smokin' he just lit me on fire! Whatever the reason was to bring us to our knees, literally, I didn't care because I was having a ton of hot, smokin', fiery, fun without a *single* rug burn!

I don't think I really need to go into the details because my parents might be reading this, but let's just say that because he was *really* nice, he slept on the hard floor and I slept on the couch after we christened Louise's new family room.

So maybe things were starting off a little out of order (actually, that was his phrase for our current situation), but I completely agreed. After all the booze, the bonus time we had together, and him sleeping on the floor, it would be unbelievable to think he would have actually called me two days later. I remember the quiet, little portion of the late night when he programmed my number into his cell phone and I remember thinking, 'Awe, he *is* nice but I won't hold my breath'. But he did call. Wow, he *was* nice.

Okay, so far so good with set-up number 2. He called like a normal guy and asked me out in a normal way, and, in some thankful way, I already had movie plans with my friend Thelma. I believe, in the rules for dating, this is what's supposed to transpire when a normal guy calls for a normal date. The dating books say to state you have plans even when you don't. *Ridiculous.* However, I was way too inexperienced to know this at the time which is probably my own, personal irony of life and the reason why he chose to call me the following day in the first place. Dating can be so much more successful when you're clueless.

So, the next weekend, we were headed for our first date to the movies and I was so excited. I tried to play it off to my mom like it was no big deal but of course she wanted to know every play by play and the itinerary of my evening *before* I even got there!

"Why are you driving to him?" she asked.

"I dunno, mom. I just am."

"Where are you going with him?" she asked

"We're going to a movie and grabbing a bite to eat."

"Well are you sure this guy is safe?"

"Yeah, mom. He's safe and I'll be fine."

"Well, you're coming home, right? I mean, it's a long drive but you're coming home, right? Don't have more than one drink!"

"I guess I'm coming home. What do you think, mom, that I'm gonna sleep with him on our first date?"

What a piece of shit I was for playing my mom like that. Had she'd known about the carpet coaster I was on last weekend, she would have been speechless!

"I'll be fine. I promise. He's a *really* nice guy. Really."

I think that put her at ease and I called her as I was pulling into his driveway just to hold her over for a bunch of hours. Maybe, just maybe, I could talk to her tomorrow- *after 9am!*

I had to keep reminding myself that I *was* a grown woman. The fact that I felt pressured to explain myself to my mom at 34 years old was making me a little uncomfortable. I completely understood her concern and skepticism but maybe I needed a little space. I've never minded sharing intimate details with my mom. She wasn't born yesterday and I'm convinced she had some Sister Christian moments upon escaping from catholic school way back when. She always gave me the real deal, never sugar-coating anything. Sometimes it hurt, maybe even stung, but I always felt grateful for her honesty even when I showed it in a crying temper tantrum. However, at this moment, I was feeling the need for a little space to explore something without her interference…yet.

We did get that bite to eat and had a beer or two before wandering over to the movie theater. I felt relaxed and happy and sort of stunned that I was actually sitting there with him. We found some end seats in the theater and the lights went out. The movie was horrible! At first, we sat through the first part of the movie truly interested. Julianne Moore was lighting up the screen and the story was getting suspenseful. I was feeling a little nervous about the plot and comfortably took his hand. He held my hand, stroking and caressing it like silk. I seemed to have been giving him the chills as my nails gently scratched the surface of his palm. The tension was building in the movie and the tension was building in our seats. We were snuggled closer and closer, legs pressed together and hands entwined and then it happened! Julianne Moore was attacked by aliens! Aliens? How *stupid*.

Why would the director ruin a perfectly good movie with the sudden onset of *aliens*. My date and I looked at each other and knowingly knew it was time to cut it loose. Our eyes locked and we embraced in a perfectly matched make- out and then we left. We left the aliens, walked outside, noticed the lunar eclipse, and let the energy of the moon take over at his apartment. I have to say, his bed was way more comfortable than the carpet, however, our extremely hot chemistry wouldn't have minded where we were.

The remainder of the night was near perfection. Candles were lit, a little Bad Company playing in the background singing "Feel Like Makin' Love", which I thought was quite apropos. We completely lost track of time and I felt lost in a place I had never been, far from my comfort zone, not thinking once about where I should be or needed to be, because I was exactly where I wanted to be; underneath, on top, and all over the place with this smokin' body of a man!

The following day I totally fibbed to my mother's face. I felt tremendously guilty about that, knowing how worried she always is about me, but I had to feel like a grown-up every once in a while. So I fibbed. *A little*.

"Did you come home last night?" she asked with raised eyebrows.

"No. It was late. We had a bite to eat, saw a movie, and then grabbed a few beers. I wasn't very comfortable to drive 45 minutes home so I crashed at his place."

More eyebrows, awaiting clarification.

"Mom, he was a total gentleman and he slept on the couch! He let me sleep in the bed and he slept on the couch. I swear". Fingers crossed behind my back. I felt like I just got busted with my first pack of cigarettes, *'they're not mine, I swear!'*

"Really. He slept on the couch? And you slept in the bed? Really?", totally not believing me. If there is anyone in this entire universe that can see directly through my soul, it's my own mother.

"Really, mom. Really."

"Well I told you to have *one* drink".

"I know mom, I know. It's all fine and I'm not the missing picture on the back of a milk carton. It's fine."

If she wanted me to believe that it was about the one-drink warning, I let her believe it but I think she secretly let me off the hook and we never spoke of it again because we really didn't have to. She knew. She always does. Luckily, there were many, many more dates to come so it became quite obvious to anyone that knew me, including my parents, that I was happily having sex on a regular basis.

In fact, besides the obvious sleepovers and the awesome dates, he was calling me religiously everyday, usually more than once. He actually told me he, either liked hearing my voice, or missed hearing my voice. I took either excuse for him calling. I was loving it! Then the text messaging started in between the phone calls. More fun. We were seeing each other pretty much once or twice a week, talking everyday and every night. I was really becoming attached to his late night phone call. I eagerly awaited it, having already washed my face, brushed my teeth and hopped into bed. He was the last person I spoke to before I closed my eyes for many hours and it made me feel like he was getting frozen inside my brain until I opened my eyes again. I don't think I was acting weird, I was just feeling very comforted with this routine. If that was the closest I could come to curling up to him every night before I closed my eyes, then so be it.

Could I possibly say the word "boyfriend", because that's how it was starting to feel, although I would never dare to speak that sacred, yet petrifying word. We dated our way through the fall, falling for each other with the season and were heading into a tricky time of year, our birthdays (1 day apart), and Christmas time. This meant gift giving, family obligations, children commitments, and, the exes.

The birthday thing was beautiful. I never get to have a really good birthday celebration because it's always so close to Thanksgiving and everyone is dealing with family, travel, or they're just simply pooped and full-bellied from the actual holiday. I guess he understood that, too, seeing as though our birthdays were so close. We went out for a really nice dinner and exchanged safe but special gifts which were very endearing and sweet. We celebrated the remainder of the night in our own little birthday bubble, way on top of the mountain in his warm and welcoming apartment.

On came the holidays which were a little more sticky, but we had a fairly good momentum going and got through it somehow. Between the Christmas parties and the shopping and the work commitments, we did struggle to find the time to spend together. After a long and draining month of pre-holiday stress, we finally reached the climax of December. On Christmas Eve, we both found ourselves talking to each other in the driveways of our ex-spouses, recapping each others evening before our phone call and wishing each other merriness. It almost felt like we were in the throws of an affair, the way we both shivered outside, talking like secret lovers.

He bought me earrings. I don't know any other way to write it except to just blurt it out. He bought me earrings and they were very pretty and delicate and completely reflected the taste I would have imagined him to have. Maybe his friend picked them out, maybe not, but I'm going with my gut that he had the final say in what he thought I would look pretty in. He bought me earrings. He bought me other little thoughtful things too like candles and fluffy socks for my forever, cold feet. Little things like that. But, the earrings got me. I was so completely touched. I hadn't received anything special like that in a long time and I felt like I was floating in the clouds and I never took them off. I figured it must be getting more serious since jewelry was now involved. *That was a stupid thought. Back to that later.*

I didn't know *what* to get him, so I wrote him a very special poem, framed it, and wrapped it up. I am very good at expressing myself with words and anything that lends itself to being creative, so I took the personal plunge on a poem. Because our time together was fairly scheduled and often limited, I wanted to give him the gift of free time, no worries and no responsibilities. I decided to take him to my beach house.

Not the most romantic place in January considering it's cold, empty, and desolate. But we made it work with a crackling fire, a furry blanket, and some body heat.

When we arrived after a leisurely drive along the LIE in January, it was such a surprise to walk into a place that was completely prepared with everything we might need for an evening alone. Thelma had taken a drive out the day before with all the "supplies" that would provide us with a romantic evening. He had never been there, so the whole place was new to him. But as I looked around, I was so taken back with all the special touches Thelma had left for us. There was firewood stacked by the fireplace ready for a cold, January night, candles all about and ready to be lit, wine and glasses ready on the coffee table waiting to be filled, snacks of shrimp and cheese on a pretty spread in the fridge. Massage oil was left by the nightstand for whatever we wanted to massage, Peter Gabriel was left by the CD player which was what we had listened to many times before, and, most importantly, the heat had been turned on, leaving the house warm and inviting. Perfection for the Christmas gift that I didn't know how to give. My friend, she helped me create a magical Christmas present and I'm not sure I could ever thank her properly in this lifetime.

After munching on our private stash of shrimp cocktail, and having a couple of drinks to get relaxed, we killed some time before our dinner reservations. We definitely developed a new appreciation for an over-sized chair with pent up energy and anticipation. It's amazing what a 2-hour drive, a couple of beers, and pretty panties can do! I finally headed upstairs to the shower to get myself ready for a lovely dinner. It was weird getting ready start to finish with him around. He has only seen me finished before we went out. Now, I was blow drying my hair and putting on my make up with him in the shower. It felt so natural and I knew I was doomed because anything that felt that good was bound to come to a screeching halt at some point.

Later on, I took him out to dinner at a wonderful steak place, busy with local patrons and amazing food. We waited in the busy bar while our table was being prepared and had a pre-dinner drink. We kissed and canoodled and didn't seem to have a care in the world. When our table was ready we sat side by side, talking and laughing and sharing side orders of creamed spinach and hash browns with our steak. We watched people, talked about our girls, and just seemed to be enjoying each others presence. At least, that's how I perceived the evening. I can only hope deep within my soul that he felt that way, too.

We returned to have a beautiful night, completely alone, a fire burning, and music playing. The rest.... is private. It was extremely intimate with only the firelight lighting our way other than the familiarity we had for each other's bodies. We found the beat of each song, changing up the rhythm each time. I thought that was really the best gift of all. Honestly, it was one of my best nights ever and maybe a gift to me, as well.

Things got a little rocky after the New Year, probably because I was feeling more attached to him, but we figured it out and we got back on track by the end of winter. I was definitely feeling strongly about him but he was a "take it slow" kind of guy and that was surely going to kill me. I'm the kind of person that when I feel something or know something, or whatever, I just want to go for it. I knew I loved him. I knew it from the moment he brought an ice cream sundae to bed one late night. How can I not fall in love with man who makes a loaded sundae and brings it back to bed while I'm wearing his shirt and nothing else *and* feeds me bites? I was in love. I didn't tell him, though. It was very hard to keep that to myself, because when you finally feel that way, you just want to scream it to the world. Instead, I screamed for ice cream and left it at that. For the first time in my life, I *really* had to keep my big mouth shut for this *really* nice guy. However I kept opening it a little for an occasional bite of our ice cream sundae.

The summer came upon us and we enjoyed cooking together, watching movies, and sitting on the hammock looking out at the tremendous view from his mountain-top apartment. We shared a beautiful 4th of July, staring at the fireworks exploding all over the Hudson Valley from on top of the mountain and taking pictures of the gorgeous sunset. We just leaned out over the towering balcony in a comfortable silence, feeling the body heat of each other as the wind whipped from such a high altitude. I had never felt so at peace with someone in my life. Then, we broke up.

Yes, we broke up at the end of the summer. Apparently, we weren't progressing. We were still holed up alone together, not meeting each others friends, family, kids, nothing. *And*...I still loved him but I hadn't said a word. I *really* fell hard for the *really* nice guy. It's funny because everyone wants to have a *really* nice guy. The problem with a *really* nice guy is that they are too nice to want to hurt you in anyway. The problem with that is it makes them look like a coward, as though they've been stringing you along so they didn't have to be "un-nice". The *really* nice guy doesn't like any confrontation whatsoever, and therefore, will avoid a fight at any cost, even if it means canceling plans when a hint of hostility is suspected over the phone. The *really* nice guy wants to talk and share endlessly about his kids but doesn't want you to spend any time with them. The *really* nice guy doesn't *really* want to let you go but doesn't *really* know what he wants to do with you either.

So we broke up. I sincerely thought this guy was the "one". I thought about the endless phone calls, text messages, fabulous intimacy, the uninhibited sex, the time invested, and the earrings. I don't know, I guess I wanted more than him at the wrong time. I always tell people that if they want to know what bad-timing looks like in the dictionary, look it up and there will be my face splashed across the page! Seriously, I have the worst timing of anyone I ever knew. Maybe I should start trying to time my timing. That would go against the laws of fate, wouldn't it? Believe me, if I thought for a second that I could be a little happier, I would give it a shot.

Anyway, my heart didn't ache a little from this one. My heart was completely and utterly broken. Talk about a break! When I took a break from online dating, I didn't think it would be an actual *break*. I was suffering from insufferable heartbreak and I didn't know how to get back on track. I cried more over this man than I did my own ex-hole (interesting reflection). This man was everything my ex was not. He was so similar to my dad and I always heard that girls are attracted to men that remind them of their father. I was confused that my ex-husband never did, but now I realize that I wasn't supposed to be with him in the end anyway.

This guy.... just like my dad. I was so sold on that, like it was a sign. I figured, every couple has a rocky patch or two or three or twenty, its life. Well, I guess he wasn't *really* ready. He was *really* nice but not *really* ready. I told him I loved him. I figured my ship was going down anyway, I might as well be as honest as I could be and be true to my own feelings. I think my heart knew at that point that he didn't love me back and so I wasn't too shocked when he just hugged me tight and told me everything *except* that he loved me too.

I'm not regretful about that night. I'm glad he knew how I felt when he left my house. I'm glad he knew he could be loved again after the break up of his own marriage and, at the same time, I'm glad he knew that he strung me along far enough that I did fall in love with him. Shame on him. I guess you have to watch out for those *really* nice guys with kids and smokin' bodies, because they cause heartbreak, too. I wasn't sure what I was more disgusted with…him, or the idea that my website was waiting for me in the wings like a rebound relationship!

Notes to self:
Really nice guys are still just…guys.
Never "take a break" for granted because some actually hurt.

Contestant #4

Well....I came back to my website. My "break" was over in more ways than one. My "break" had a three time sting since I logged off a while back and seemed to have gotten worse with every step forward I had thought I was making. I knew, however, that if I didn't do something after this last (heart) break, I would fall into a spiraling sea of depression, drowning in the floods of my own tears. Okay, that's a little dramatic, but I was starting to look like shit. I think there is something deep to consider when you fall asleep crying and actually wake up crying. It doesn't sound possible but it really is! I had to find the strength to get back up on the dating horse, no matter what ride I was going to get.

I punched at the keyboard and entered my screen name and password to find my old self staring back at me. It was like the picture of myself was looking at me and chanting *'Mirror mirror on the wall, who's the dumbest girl of all?'*

It actually didn't take long to get hit on again which was encouraging. Contestant #4 had a nice picture, although he did sport a baseball cap in his photos. He had a nice, friendly smile and I found communication came really easy with him via email, for a while. We spoke on the phone a few times upon graduating from email; however, I think I might have been losing interest after that. When I email with someone, it's often hard to hear tone, nervousness, and any other communication traits that I normally immediately sense in person. When I graduated to the phone calls, I started to pick up on the things that remained conveniently absent during the emails such as tone, sarcasm, lulls, or even cluelessness. I often type like I speak and, therefore, I can get a sense from the other person's typing as well. Maybe that's too assuming on my part or even an excuse to be too quick to judge. Maybe the typing efforts weren't the real problem at all. Maybe I was just forcing myself into something I probably wasn't feeling ready for quite yet. Maybe it just came down to the fact that I wasn't feeling much connection to #4 at this point. However, I just got back on this damn website so I wasn't about to nix the 1ˢᵗ potential date I've had in a long while. I sucked it up. Besides, we already invested time into numerous emails and a couple of calls. *Why not?*

Contestant #4 lived about a town or two away and we decided to meet at the tavern down the street from my house. I wasn't thrilled with that idea because I often knew plenty of people in that tavern at any given time. However, it was a week night and I sort of hoped I wouldn't run into anyone I might've known.

I arrived at the tavern about 5 minutes late and, of course, walked into a full bar. Stupid me knew it was a week night but it was also a Thursday night, and that's a pretty busy night at a local tavern! Obviously, I really had no idea who I was looking for which left me to walk in, look around, and *want* to see someone I knew. The other dates I had met were under quieter circumstances and easy to seek out. This guy was going to be like finding a needle in a haystack. As I was looking around, naturally I ran into a couple of guys that I knew from high school. I was a little relieved by that but I knew it would put me in an awkward position in a matter of minutes. I hadn't seen them in a while so we were pretty jazzed to run into each other. The small talk was riddled with smiles and laughs and then came the inevitable question….

"Who are you meeting here?" *Duhhh.*

I guess this moment brings me back to the beginning of my worries when one of my nervous questions was *'what if I run into people I know?'* *What was I supposed to answer?* Any second this blind date from the internet was going to walk in and I was going to have to fess up in some way. *Or,* maybe the guy was already here and I didn't see him yet. Maybe, he was watching *me!* I decided to be truthful, sort of. I told my old friends that I was about to meet a blind date. Someone set me up. I mean, life *was* setting me up in some way; probably for huge embarrassment. I really didn't want to get into the internet thing so I was only partially truthful. It didn't matter because they got a kick out of that anyway.

Once I got past the awkwardness and the chuckling of my impending date, I felt the sudden need to turn around. It must've been my cricket yelling at me inside my head. I turned towards the door and noticed a very little guy looking around, as if searching for someone. Since it was clear that everyone in the place had someone to talk to, I concluded that this must be my date. I immediately noticed that he left his baseball cap at home. I wish he hadn't. Not only was he tiny (like I had a solid 50 pounds on him), but he was bald like an older gentleman with a ring of hair around the lower half of his head. Kind of like a Robert Duvall hair style. I did recognize some of his facial features that confirmed to me that this was indeed the guy.

For a slight, split second, I thought of walking out the backdoor. Ugh, how mean. I could never do that. I felt bad watching him look around for me so I decided to do the right thing. I said bye to the guys as they did their very best to lean around and check this guy out. I quickly introduced myself to #4 and whisked him out and across the street to the high-fiving bar! As we walked across the intersection, I pleasantly explained that it was jammed in there and so loud. #4 seemed instantly relieved with my quick thinking and we entered the small, little bar that I met presumptuous Chinese food guy a few contestants ago.

We entered the bar and found a little cocktail table to perch at for a bit. I ordered my standard red wine and he ordered........sprite. *Uh-oh.* There is something about a non-drinking guy that sends my flag up. I don't know why. There really isn't anything wrong with someone who chooses not to drink. I guess I just wished I knew that *before* I ordered mine. I could've had a seltzer or something.

"So, you're a teacher." He confirmed with me.

"Yeah, I teach reading." I reconfirmed from a past phone conversation.

"So, the place was busy across the street?" he continued.

"It really was. It didn't look like there would be any place for us to sit or hear each other." I added.

Not like the conversation required a quiet table or anything.

"Did you know anyone in there? Across the street?" he asked.

"I did run into a couple of old high school buddies for a few minutes. I usually always run into someone somewhere."

"Oh! So you're like a popular girl." he chided.

"Well, not really, but I do live here so it's easy for me to run into people randomly." I said.

This conversation was going nowhere!

In some ways it was the fastest glass of wine I had had in a long time. I think I knew this by the speed of the message my hand was sending to the stem of my glass. We had little to talk about, even less than on the phone, which I had already sensed from our phone conversations and that was probably the reasoning behind my hand having a drinking mind of its own. I felt like Contestant #4 and I slowly used up any conversation we had from email, to phone, to person. By the time we actually sat across from each other, there was nothing left to say. The conversation had runneth dry, and so did my wine glass. Aside from that main point, I also knew I wasn't attracted to #4 because I couldn't get passed the part that he had old man hair and an 8th graders body. *Last gulp.* Contestant #4 was over.

Notes to self:
Never assume a full head of hair under a baseball cap
Conversations can have a lull or an emptiness; *know the difference!*

Contestant #5

Okay so balding, baseball cap guy didn't really work out past the 'hello' part but I was getting more hits on the website which was a little encouraging. I was still stinging over the idea of being back on this thing again anyway, not really knowing for sure whether I was ready or not (probably not). I knew I didn't have much of a choice. My best friend had used up her two set-up choices on me and probably wasn't scrambling around to find me more heartache. Maybe she needed a *break* from my dating, too! My other friends didn't have anyone to set me up with and, frankly, I was more convinced than ever that set-up meant being framed for disappointment or simply just something that people feel they need to do with any single person they know. Contrary to my apparent negative feelings about being set-up, I think being set-up *has* to be better than online dating only because at least the set-ee has been somewhat screened through your friends, while, the online guy has only been screened by the website that he's *paying*. Whatever, no set-ups at the moment anyway so let's go out with Contestant #5 from the Bronx!

What is interesting about Contestant #5 was that he actually impressed me enough to make it to a second date which I hadn't felt compelled to do since Contestant #1. The first time we met seemed easy going and calm. We met for a drink in Eastchester, which we decided was our half way point. *That went well, I thought. Was he my type? Not sure.* I didn't think so but he was very nice and quite attentive towards me and I think maybe I was enjoying myself a little. We fumbled through a lot of small talk about the obvious way in which we met. A couple of tidbits of our past relationships were thrown in there for good measure. And, reflecting back, he asked more questions about me than the amount of information he offered up about himself. Pretty smart on his part, considering our second date.

When we ended up saying goodbye that evening, we had made a definite decision to go out again very soon. In fact, I believe we went out to dinner the following weekend.

"Ohhhhh, second date" my friends chided.

"What does he do?"

"What does he look like?"

"Was he nice?"

"Did he pay?"

"Where are you going next?"

I answered, "Yes, not sure, not bad, yes, yes, dinner."

They were so curious about the guy that possibly won me over on a second date after the trauma of Break #3.

"I'm really not sure if this guy's for me" I adamantly replied. I really *did* feel that way but I also knew I owed it to myself *and* to him to get together for dinner and really make an effort to get to know him. So I did.

We met at a restaurant in Mamaroneck, set back from the main street bustle. It was a pretty place lit up with Christmas lights in the plants. I could tell it was a little over the top in the décor department but it was pretty, clean, and had a very friendly atmosphere. Maybe *too* friendly.

Apparently, Contestant #5 knew the owners quite well and we were getting service and attention that was almost as over the top as the Italian décor! Contestant #5 was waiting at the bar for me, chatting with the bartender who seemed like an old pal of kind. I walked in, he took my coat and handed me a…..big, pink rose. It was very sweet but a little awkward for me.

I was gracious by smelling it, "It's beautiful. Thank you." *Was I supposed to carry this rose through the restaurant now? Was everyone going to see me carrying a lone flower and make the correct, yet humiliating, assumption that this was our first date?* I felt kind of silly to tell the truth. I suppose if I were to receive flowers, a delivery to my house is most comfortable either, by the giver or by the delivery truck.

So we walked through the restaurant and, as I suspected, people looked at me adoringly (mostly the older Italians who probably eat there every night, dining on the chefs daily specials), knowing that their dear Italian Stallion was taking me to dinner in their place of marinara worship. Kind of like a "Go Team" feeling. The funny thing was, these people probably didn't even know him but they were rallying behind him anyway because their ancestors shared a country at some point in history.

So we were seated in a corner by candlelight and I was feeling a little pressured to enjoy every second. As I stared at the murals of ivy climbing the walls and gondolas sailing through the plaster, I thought maybe I would have rather gone to a pub for a burger and a beer.

Contestant #5 ordered us a bottle of wine but I already made the mental note to have only one glass. We had the specials recited to us by a very attentive male waiter and we decided on sharing an appetizer and having our own entrees. I have to say, it wasn't an awful night however, maybe just not my idea of a fun-getting-to-know-you type atmosphere. Although this restaurant was without the noisy crowd and live music, I think I got to know enough of him over dinner, seeing as though I hadn't learned much about him on our first date.

"So what exactly is the type of job you have, because it wasn't very specific in your profile?" I asked.

"Well", he replied, "my family owns a couple of companies in the Bronx." (*Flag*)

"Oh yeah? What kind of companies?"

"Uh, we own a paving company and also a few motels."

"Oh", I said, thinking about that last part of his statement (*RED FLAG!*).

"So, when you get up in the morning, what job do you get dressed to do?" I inquired, feeling a *little* confused with his cautious and evasive approach.

"Well, I don't really get up in the morning. I usually sleep until the early afternoon because I work the night shifts at the motels."

I could feel my eyebrows rising into my forehead with that feeling of surprise laced with curiosity, and sprinkled with *Holy Crap*.

"Oh." Now I was starting to wonder if I had ever even *seen* a motel in the Bronx and if I had, did people actually *choose* to stay in a motel in the Bronx? (*RED WAVING FLAG!*)

"Okay, so you work the night shift every night, isn't that a little scary?" I asked innocently.

"Yeah, which is why I have a gun."

He looked at me as though waiting for some kind of reaction about the gun. I had nothing except that now my eyebrows were stuck atop of my forehead with no hopes of coming back down to my mildly bulging eyeballs! (*RED WAVING FLAG WITH SIRENS!*)

Am I supposed to knock the guy for carrying a little protection with him to his job? Hmmm, instead I just chose to knock back the rest of the wine to aide me through the remainder of this conversation.

"So when you are working, what do you do there?" I asked.

"Basically I do the books and the billing and keep an eye on all the security cameras. I have a lot of cash with me in the office which is why I feel safer with the gun."

"Oh."

I mean, of course, a lot of cash. Because who is using their American Express Corporate Account to pay for a motel in the Bronx? In fact, what kind of people actually stay there that do pay cash? I already had some pretty good guesses. My mind started racing and I was almost wishing to backtrack this conversation to where he might have said that he was a paver instead! Maybe his family was also in the sanitation business, too! **(*FLAG! FLAG! FLAG!*)**

Well this whole conversation took a turn into awkward land over dessert.

"So, I had a really nice time with you, Jacey." Contestant #5 said.

"Me too. The food was really good. It was a nice evening." I said safely.

"Thanks again for the pretty rose." I added for good measure.

"It was my pleasure. I saw it and thought of you."

Bleh. Too sappy for me.

I sipped on a cup of coffee to help erase the remnants of the wine and also because I knew I would be on the phone late tonight replaying this evening with my friends. My rose was lying there, beginning to wilt, kind of like this date. I knew I couldn't do it. I couldn't do the gun (unless he was a cop), I couldn't do the night shifts, I couldn't do the sleeping all day thing, and I definitely couldn't do the explanation of Bronx motels to my parents. I could just see them now, trying to explain *that* to their golfing group over dinner at the country club! I retrieved my eyebrows back off the top of my forehead, composed myself, and thanked him for a lovely evening. Contestant #5 was over.

Notes to self:
Occupations should be *clearly* defined in the profile!
Guns for jobs are *only* okay for law enforcement!

Contestant #6

So that last Contestant was a funny laugh for everyone I knew. Of course, since I made it to a second date with that guy, everyone wanted to know "how it went". It went. It went right into the Bronx motel dumpster with a bunch of rats and missing business invoices! I felt bad because Contestant #5 meant well, I could tell. Perhaps I was being a bit too picky or I was relying too much on instant attraction, but I really felt compelled to go with my gut during this experience and, as Paula Abdul says to the American Idol contestants, "stay true to yourself". I think I mentioned in the beginning of this book that online dating *did* seem like an online game show. I stayed true like Paula says. I wasn't into him, or the flower, or the motels, or the gun, or another date.

It's during this part of the post-date that gets a little uncomfortable because it was time to break the connection, in this particular case, the phone connection since that was the only initial connection we really had. I was never one to have many boyfriends growing up. I had a lot of guy pals and a couple of quality insurance policies when a girl needed a little extra attention now and then. It was a decent understanding, one that served its purpose many times over. My point is, I never really had to do much breaking up stuff because there wasn't much reason to. Except now there was and I really had no idea how to do it except for the cowardly way. I guess I figured that since we met online, we could un-meet online. Fair enough? Probably not but this was already a big enough adjustment as it was and I didn't have time for a "breaking up online-101" class.

Anyway, I jumped onto the website, located his previous email from me, stating what a great time he had and asking when we were doing it again. Rats! He wasn't making this any easier besides the fact that I was already feeling like a total snobby bitch because I didn't like his choice of career or business. I took a deep breath, thought about my words carefully because I didn't want to come across as unkind or like that snobby bitch I knew I could be deep, down inside. I typed off a short email about *what a nice dinner we had and how thoughtful he was but, that, after all that conversation, it had become clear to me that maybe we didn't have that much in common after all.*

I thought it sounded pretty okay and I suppose he did too because he just gracefully wished me well and we said goodbye. If he hadn't been lingering around my personal space for so long when he walked me to my car, I would think he didn't dig me so much but I know he really wanted to lay one on me! Sorry motel guy. The truth was, we really *didn't* have anything in common after all so I wasn't going to beat myself up over the other stuff.

After I finished my Dear John letter to Contestant #5, I checked my messages for any new prospects. Low and behold!! There was Contestant #6. This guy was nice looking and had a successful job. We immediately started exchanging lots of emails and he was a chatty little thing. Coming from me, who *is* a chatty little thing, he emailed my ear off. But, I did like the conversation and we were never at a loss for words.

Eventually, we graduated to the phone at a fairly quick clip and had a number of phone chats over the next few weeks. We talked about everything from jobs, to kids, to exes. The weird thing about Contestant #6 was his compulsion to ask the most nitty, gritty, detailed questions. He would ask intimate questions, ultimatum questions, what-if questions, and he was constantly pop quizzing me on my own profile. His phone calls were mostly filled with him asking and me answering, or explaining, or elaborating. Interesting twist; from a guy. *Was he generally interested or was he extremely paranoid?*

I decided to 86 all this pop quiz crap and suggest the idea of grabbing a drink. I felt like if I had one more phone chat with this guy and had to answer one more question, we would never make it to a first date.

"Let's meet", I said spontaneously.

"Let's just grab a drink and hang out together instead of using up all this fine conversation over the phone", I kept on.

He happily agreed, so I concluded that maybe it was possible that he was nervous to suggest it in the first place or something.

We decided to meet at a chic restaurant in Mt. Kisco that I was always fond of. I never had a bad meal there, the service was great, and I always saw somebody famous! Contestant #6 had just moved to the area after his divorce so it was very convenient for him, to say the least. I took the ten minute drive which was completely fine with me.

I met him on a Friday evening so he was still in his work suit and sported somewhat of a commuter smell consisting of city cab smog mixed with day old cologne, splashed with overcrowded train. It was fine and my hound dog snout adjusted to the nice looking face that stared back at me.

We met at the bar, he took my coat off for me, and he bought me a drink. *Nice.* We sat close, catching up and, then, the questions started again! It was like a giant repeat of all the phone conversations all wrapped up and jarbled together! *Hadn't I already answered these questions?* I was suddenly starting to feel as though I was being interrogated.

"So you're a teacher?"

"What grade?"

"And do you like it? Do you think it was your 'calling'?"

"How long have you been divorced?"

"He left you, right?"

"Why did he leave you?"

"But you have 2 girls, correct?"

"How old are they again?"

"So what do you like to do on your off time?"

"You have a lot of friends?"

"Are they single or married?"

"Have you been going out a lot?"

"How's this internet thing working for you?"

"Any good matches yet?"

"You grew up locally, didn't you say?"

"About 10 minutes from here, right?"

It went on and on. After summing up much of the personal information that was already covered in one of our many phone chats, Contestant #6 said, "Have you ever come here for the after hours gig they have?"

"Uh, I don't think so, I have only been here for pre-dinner drinks and dinner", I replied.

In a semi-whispered voice he said "Well, I've heard they have a pretty happening situation going on here late night", he edged in closer.

"Liiike?" I drawled.

I mean, if you have something to say, then just spit it out for goodness sake.

"I heard they have a whole after-hour porn thing going on that they put on the bar TV's", he informed me with the raise of his eyebrows.

I was waiting for him to move his eyebrows up and down like Bert. *Was he implying or questioning (as he clearly does) if I would be into that????*

"Oh", I said. "I can't actually say I've ever heard that rumor about this place. Kind of hard to imagine!"

He led on that he was as surprised to hear about the rumor as I was but I knew he couldn't wait to tell me all about it even though he didn't know me from a hole in the wall.

We floated through the porn topic pretty quickly because I wasn't offering up anymore for that portion for date #6. As far as I was concerned, that was just down right weird 1ˢᵗ date conversation. *Weird.*

"I'm starving!" he announced. "I haven't eaten since lunch, you hungry?" he asked.

"Um, I could eat a little something. I'm not starving but I could pick", I replied. Judging by his earlier excitement about bar porn, I thought for sure we would be ordering appetizers at the bar. *But Nooooooo!*

"Let me check with the host and see if he can grab us a table", and he walked towards the door.

Damn, I didn't want a table. I was happy just roosting in my bar space, a table always seems more intimate or date-ish or something. I looked around and there were plenty of small tables surrounding the bar and scattered about so I thought maybe one of those would be fine and it wouldn't kill the atmosphere I had gotten used to. *But Nooooooo!*

"Okay, grab your drink, the host has a nice table for us upstairs", #6 informed me when he returned to the bar.

Upstairs was just the bigger dining room of this place. It was a pretty room, painted with dark red walls, tiny votive candles flickering on each table, and wrought iron artwork scattered about on the walls. The tables were on the closer side of each other and there were tables backed up to dark red banquets, providing a more intimate dining experience for those who like to cuddle and eat….It was on the darker side, providing plenty of ambience, and it was separated from the rest of the restaurant; like the bar, the place I felt comfortable.

Oh well, I grabbed my drink, he grabbed my coat and followed. He *did* have nice manners. Had it not been for the porn plug, I might have really decided to like him right away, but that other little thing was nagging at me like a thong that doesn't fit right!

We climbed the tall stairs and we were led to a small table in the corner (*of course*) where it was particularly dark, uncrowded, and backed up to a banquette. *Jeez, always these dark, private tables in the corners!* Anyway, we ordered. He got a full meal and I got a salad and an appetizer.

Guys can eat whatever, whenever, in front of whoever. It's very amusing to watch. Also, without having to ask too many things, you can pick up some interesting information about a guy when he orders something. The way he scopes the menu, asks questions, grills the server, orders for his date, or just the plain old arrogant attitude that many display while being waited on. That attitude is the worst. The attitude that allows the customer to *think* he is better than the server because *he* is the one being waited on. *And,* it doesn't always have to be a 'he'. 'She's' do it too! Having been a waitress for a small portion of my life, I notice these things.

Contestant #6 was very polite to the server and, ironically, didn't drill her with questions like I expected him to. I guess the drilling and grilling session was only reserved for me. He confidently ordered a seafood dish and I was thinking that fish would be an interesting smell to add to the commuter smell. *Hmmm.*

So we were sitting side by side at a table of four backed up into a cushy couch banquette. Talk about close quarters, but at least we weren't *next* to each other on the banquette. We were chatting some more and I was still finding myself answering his freaking questions. If any of my close friends were ever questioned about me, they would easily confirm that I hate being fired upon with question after question. The funny thing is, I'll pretty much talk about anything but it's hard to have or carry a conversation when you are being brutally interrogated. I veered off and tried to turn the table.

"So how is your new condo?" I asked.

"Oh it's really nice. It's actually down the road from here and I'm moving in the rest of my stuff this weekend". He continued, "I think it needs a little work, like some fresh paint which is no big deal, but I might take down a wall and open up one of the rooms to be a bit bigger".

"Wow, that sounds like a project but I guess if you're starting a new phase in your life, start it the way you really want to - if you can", I added.

We talked some more about the new phases of life that seem to come unexpectedly such as divorce, new dwellings, visitation and then finally the food came. He ate with nice manners, as though he had been accustomed to restaurants for a long time or his parents taught him well. The date seemed easy until he plugged that damn porn again.

"So, you mean to tell me that you live around here and you have *never* heard about the (whisper) porn thing at this place?" (*Ugh!*)

"No, I really have *never* heard about the (whisper) porn in this place. Really. Truly. Honestly", I insisted.

"That surprises me." he said.

I'm sorry, did I look like a porn worshipper?

"Why does it surprise you that I'm not aware of the after hour's stuff here?" I asked, truly curious of his answer.

"I dunno, I guess since you live around here and you've been dating I thought maybe you would have heard about it, for sure. Just surprised you haven't. That's all."

"Oh." Was all I could muster up.

"How's your dinner?" he asked, wiping his mouth with his napkin.

"It's good. I like the food here."

"Because you come here a lot and yet you've never heard about the porn. Funny." He added.

I really didn't feel like getting grilled anymore on my potential knowledge of this situation and I was anticipating that more was coming because, as we know, #6 *loves* to ask questions. I decided to shift gears in a hurry. We were pretty much finished with our meal so I knew this date would be winding down soon.

"How big is your condo that you could actually knock a wall down?" I asked.

I wasn't really interested but I was too afraid of getting backed into the porner corner.

"Oh", he started with enthusiasm. He started moving our plates out of the way to the other side of the table.

"Here's the layout", he began.

He started using the utensils to diagram a map of the condo. He marked off different rooms with forks, knives, and spoons and was trying to show me how it looked. He banged down the salt shaker and marked off the fireplace and started to explain where he was putting all his furniture. I really wasn't following and could care less but I was nodding with interest because he was excited *and* he hadn't asked me any questions in the last 4 or 5 sentences, so that was a plus. I tried to keep it going because I wanted to make sure the porn thing wasn't going to pop up again, or anything else, for that matter.

Honestly, I asked "I don't understand how you get into this place. You have walls here and furniture there, where's the door?"(*Although, I might have just opened up the door to disaster.*)

Remember I mentioned close quarters? And the banquette? Well, with my height and the mixture of the sinking banquette underneath me, it put some of my body parts perfectly level with the edge of the table. #6 began pointing to the utensils and talking me through the lay out and, like he was saving the best for last, he moved his pointing finger closer to the edge of the table and said....

"The door's right here, right here where your nipple is." *What!* I just looked at him with that *are you kidding* kind of grin. The look that had my eyes stirring wildly in their sockets while my mouth was trying to stay composed in somewhat of a grin. I then looked down toward my sacred, little nipple and mentally confirmed that he was dangerously close to it so I slowly removed my body from the edge of the table and decided to sit back in the banquette. It's not like I had my girls resting on the edge of the table or that my nipples are so gigantic that they were grazing the edge of my dinner plate. *Holy shit!*

So I shifted again. I was afraid that, after his nipple- noticing, my move backwards might come across as too inviting on a cushy surface, so I sat up straight, nipples far from the edge, and kept my cool. I don't think I've ever had a guy comment on my nipple over dinner and certainly not use it as a landmark for his condo layout.

I think this guy had crossed into weird land and the porn thing came flooding back into my brain like a big wave. Before, it was more like the ebb and flow of the tide, now the flood was here. Porn, nipples, no. I'm no prude. I like a little chemistry. I like it to be a little mutual. I like a first date to be a little less porn talk and nipple pointing out. I had a feeling that Contestant #6 had a darker side that he was trying to tease me with but all it was doing for me was freaking me (and my nipples) out. I wasn't feeling anything but his nice manners, up until his map demonstration. Not nice manners. Contestant #6 was over.

Notes to self:
Being grilled doesn't work for anything but a barbeque.
There is a time, a place, and an intuition to
even *consider* bringing up "porn".

A Break- Take 4

After this last round of dating, all *three* dates, I thought maybe I needed another break to get my thoughts and priorities in tact. I wasn't sure what my thoughts were, maybe that I *was* being too picky and I wasn't sure what my priorities were, maybe that I had no priorities and needed some. I truly believed that my priorities were to stick with my gut and not sell myself short on the matches that didn't connect. I just wanted to take a break even though my last "break" didn't go over so well. Maybe just a mental break.

I was well into the fall of autumn again and, unfortunately not falling for anyone at the present time. The last few dates had left me a little discouraged, although I was starting to appreciate the amusing side to all this online dating. Perhaps, more personal growth?

As I relayed my dating stories to my friends and family, I began realizing that people were getting quite a chuckle at my expense. It didn't bother me, in fact, it lightened up my spirits while I laughed along. It actually made me feel less nervous about going on the dates. Knowing I could possibly find some amusement in these situations was becoming a little motivating for me. I still needed a mental break from it, though.

I started a new job in a new school, teaching a new grade, and I was drowning in my new responsibilities. I had been transferred within my district due to low student enrollment. I was told I would be packing up my classroom of Legos and blocks and moving to a different school and a classroom filled with books and charts. I went from kindergarten to fourth grade in record speed and I barely had my head above water. I had no material, no knowledge, and no clue about fourth grade. I had just come from a class of tying shoes, zipping jackets, and wiping noses so I was feeling quite overwhelmed at the mere idea of getting these kids through three state tests during the year. Basically my "break" was consisting of the work priorities, the kid priorities, and the dating stories. But who had time to date anyway?

As the fall swept through the leaves, my birthday came and went, along with Thanksgiving and that small, depressing feeling that life was beginning to sweep through me as I was getting older. I should have been embracing the spirit of Thanksgiving, being thankful for a job, healthy kids, and making it to another birthday. But I *was* feeling old. I could never verbalize that complaint to any of my friends because I am the youngest out of all of them and they just pooh pooh me whenever it is mentioned. Okay, so I was feeling like the youngest oldest person of the group, but I kept it to myself! I always do. When I really thought about it, deeply, it wasn't the getting older part that necessarily bugged me, it was the idea of getting older alone every year. It was the idea that there wasn't someone who looked at me right through the birthday and saw beauty and vibrance and didn't care what age I was or what age I felt like I was. I found it depressing that I still wasn't sharing my birthday on a yearly basis with anyone. I found it depressing when I would hear the stories told by my friends about how their husbands took them here and their husbands celebrated there. How boyfriends bought them this and how boyfriends surprised them with that. I wasn't resentful because I was always happy for my friends, but I *was* feeling more and more envious.

The Christmas holidays arrived like 2 minutes after my birthday because time always seems to fly right after Thanksgiving. Everyone starts getting stressed the second Black Friday alarms go off in the dark. People are constantly walking around with the never-ending list of things to get and buy and do. Cars begin honking at people for their parking spaces when the person is taking too long in reverse. Lines in stores triple in length and cashiers move slower because half the merchandise ironically has no price tag. Coupons are being shoved into faces and scanned into registers looking for the best bargains. Fed Ex and UPS trucks speed through the small streets trying to make delivery deadlines and probably running over things in the process.

As the energy level was amped up all around me, I found myself busy shopping for my kids, making sure that their Christmas was the spectacular moment that I had developed in their little, growing brains. It had to be magical. I like making magic for them. I just had to figure out a way not to be tainted by all the Christmas chaos and crazy people that comes along with the holiday.

Time had been flying since Thanksgiving and right through Christmas. I was mildly thankful for the passing of the Christmas holiday, mostly for the same reasons of my birthday. Except with Christmas, I always had to explain to my girls some excuse as to why Santa had left nothing in my stocking or why there were no presents under the tree for me. I always simply explained that Santa still liked to deliver all my things to Mimi and Pops' house, my parents. Thankfully, they would come over for Christmas Day brunch and hand me some loot which helped reassure the girls that Santa *hadn't* forgotten about me after all.

Basically, I tried to remind myself that it was always about the kids but secretly I thought it would be nice to share it with someone else, too. As a single parent, it was always difficult to fully enjoy the good things on my own, without the endearing look of someone sitting by my side, or just simply enjoying the simple pleasures of torn wrappings everywhere. Personally, the peaceful idea of someone curled up in the dark on the living room couch with me and staring at the lit tree on Christmas Eve would've sealed the deal in my heart. I was always relieved when it was over. Then, my girls could enjoy their new things and I could get back to reality.

Thanks to teaching fourth grade, time continued to fly after the holiday break and I barely had my feet on the ground at any point in time. Anyone that does have the rare opportunity to teach this particular grade knows that the timeline of test prep and state tests makes the months shoot right by. It seemed that every month I was preparing for another test or administering another test. Every time I turned around, I was revamping my teaching schedule, pulling out another 40 pound binder and starting all over again. Of course, this was my first year at it and I was spinning around the huge professional tornado I had managed to create for myself.

So with state tests approaching in the first week of January, I was happy to go to Louise's house for New Years Eve and let off a little steam. Just a little steam because the kids were invited, too.

"Are you coming up to the house?" Louise asked.

"I sure am. The kids are psyched!"

"Good. I picked up some wine. It should be pretty quiet, though."

"That's okay. It sounds perfect to me." I assured her.

"Okay, well get going because the weather is supposed to turn crappy soon." She said.

I was happy to know that it was going to be just us with our kids, sipping wine and toasting a quiet New Year. *But, no.* I drove up north to her house, comfortable in my sweats, in a massive snow blizzard. Cars were crawling up the highway, spinning, bumping, and skidding like matchbox cars. I was very thankful for my 4-wheel drive but I was a nervous wreck that someone was going to spin, bump, or skid into me. A 45 minute trip ended up lasting 2 hours and, Lord knows, I needed a glass of wine upon arrival. My kids were petrified and I just kept distracting them by making the music louder. At certain points when I had a fleeting thought to turn back, I realized it would be pointless, and kept on trudging along.

Finally we arrived and we lugged our overnight gear inside where I was informed that every New Years straggler without plans was heading over to hang out, mostly due to the bad weather. I was just happy to be in her house where it was warm, bright, and inviting. There was wine opened and food out and music on. *Okay.* I settled in and grabbed a drink. I was happy for my sweats and my ponytail and no pressure.

As the kids ran off and I took a long awaited breather, Louise cautiously informed me that Break #3 would also be joining the straggling, New Year's festivities. *Oh crap. And,* I was still in my sweats. *Oh crap.* I tried not to show any surprise and focused all my energy on staying totally composed, like I was cool with it. As I was focusing, my mind started reeling about what I packed in that overnight bag. *Did I have deodorant in there? A brush? Different clothes?* I succumbed to the idea of wearing sweats all night because the only change of clothes I had was just another pair of sweats for the next day. The ponytail I could fix and the deodorant I could apply. I quietly ducked into the bathroom with my make-up bag and tried to fabuloutize myself before he arrived. *If* he arrived. So much for no pressure. *Wine. Take a sip.*

Well, he *did* arrive. I, of course, was a ball of nerves but I wasn't going to openly display that. He showed up with one of his daughters, saw me, walked straight toward me, kissed me hello, and the night went on. It wasn't *too* uncomfortable but I had this underlying stress oozing from every oracle of body. My girls were busy playing and weren't requiring any of my attention. Why is it that when you need the attention from your kids either to look occupied or seem distracted, they want nothing to do with you? Whatever, they were happy and that makes me happy so I got a little happier with a bottle of Shiraz.

I got myself busy and helped prepare dinner that actually seemed somewhat intimate because many of the guests hadn't come over yet. I *was* feeling a little awkward but the evening was still tinged with a mildly comfortable feeling that I was reminiscent of deep, down inside. Sometimes, it's just the absence of something that makes things seem uncomfortable, but once that gap is filled, things don't seem as awkward anymore.

Dinner was nice, with a fairly festive group gathered around the table. The kids could have cared less and dug into the chicken nuggets and fries when we put the tray out for them. They went about their important playing and the adults actually had an adult kind of time without any interruptions which was quite a treat for us all. The pressure was lower and the surrounding company was easy to be with. I ate my dinner of shrimp and angel hair and sipped my wine, while exchanging little glances with Break #3 all throughout the meal. At that point, I decided to indulge in the evening for whatever it was worth and just be content with the fate of the night.

Before I knew it, the ball was dropping in Time Square and we had all gathered around the television to see Dick count it down. My girls sat on my lap, ready to blow their New Years whistles. We counted. We counted. And we counted. *HAPPY NEW YEAR!* It always brings a little moisture to my eyes. Another year gone, and my mind raced to remember anything I might have accomplished. I looked at my girls and felt such pride of just having them next to me every minute of my life. I looked at Break #3 and he had the same mushy look in his eyes as he gazed at his daughter. *See? We get each other!* Anyway, off the girls went, grabbing another hour of play on this extremely late night for them. I wandered off into the kitchen for….more wine, but maybe just a quick change of scenery. I was feeling the New Years kissing pressure, which normally doesn't bother me except for when there's a person present that I've been longing to kiss again for months.

As it turned out, I had an unexpected follower. Break #3 followed me into the kitchen and, without hesitation, wished me a Happy New

Year with a gentle kiss on the lips and a really warm, close, tight hug. *Loved it. Damn it.*

It was that moment that I knew he and I still shared some little connection and then, later on, we connected a little bit more in a dark hallway. Thank goodness our kids were around somewhere because, no doubt, we would have found ourselves "out of order" for the second time since our initial meeting. I was feeling happy and thinking *maybe* this *was* meant to be. *Maybe the snow blizzard led us here together on purpose. Maybe he was missing me. Maybe this New Year was symbolic of a New Start. Fate?*

We continued to keep in touch for a number of months following New Years Eve with many phone calls and text messages. By the early spring, I had cautiously suggested maybe getting together for a beer or a bite or both or something. He was evasive in return. I wasn't sure if he was involved with anyone or if he just wasn't "into" me anymore or if he really was just being his overly cautious self. It could've been a little of everything. Who knows? It's funny how I had become more brave and courageous with all the online, blind dates, yet, even the mild attempt to suggest a quick burger with him was giving me some queasiness. *Him,* not the burger.

We never grabbed that burger or beer or anything. Apparently, we were grabbing chicken because he was chickening out on me, acting more afraid of what the outing could lead up to. It's not like I was going to propose to him. In pure frustration, I made a brave decision to call him up one day and invite myself over for a quick visit that night. It really had been the bravest thing I had done in a long time. Perhaps even *more* personal growth! He didn't deny me at all, and I think he really didn't mind that I was taking the bull by its horns; kind of like taking him by the hair!

So I arrived on top of the beautiful mountain once again, nervously knocked on the door, and blinked out at the view until he answered. We sat for a couple of hours, just getting used to being in the same room with each other. We chatted about safe topics, like the kids, music, and things we were already familiar about with each other. The time went fast…. for me and before I knew it, I was rising from the chair to begin the goodbye process. I didn't want to overstay my welcome, so I made the first move to end the evening. I'm sure he was thankful because let's remember, he *is* a *really* nice guy and probably wouldn't have wanted to be rude and ask me to leave.

Here came the hard part. We hugged each other tight and long and the temptation to kiss him was overwhelming me. I gently gave him a light kiss on the neck because that's where my mouth sort of lands when we hug. He looked deep in my eyes and made no move or attempt closer to my face. We were close. *Very close.* But I needed him to lean in at that point and he didn't. I looked at him so confused and questioningly. *I mean, I did remember how he enjoyed kissing me endlessly, so, why not now?* We had been communicating for quite a number of months at this point and here I was, standing in his apartment. *Why not go with the kiss?* Well, there was only so much I could stand and I felt like if our eyes didn't unlock at some point within the next 2 seconds, I was going to cry. This man was *not* going to see me cry once again.

"I just can't." he said to me regretfully. Huh? Me? Confusion. It's when someone says something stupid and the other person responds with a scrunched up face and a shake of the head? *That's how I felt,* responding to his 'I just can't'.

"Why?" I simply asked.

"It's just a can of worms. I'll call you tomorrow, okay?" he stated.

"Okay", I quietly replied. I left. He never called.

These damn breaks are killing me! No more breaks!

Was that the end of Break #3? Not quite. I had one more thing to do. Find closure. Closure has become quite an important concept, especially for girls like me who keep on getting hurt. Closure seems to verify what went wrong, justify the last actions taken, and hold the magical ability to move your emotions through any more heartache. I needed a little closure for this one.

I came home pissed off at the world with a feeling of rejection, once again. Is it fair that one person can make another feel so crappy multiple times? In teaching, it's called 'The Tour of Duty'. Like, you pay your dues and it can't, or shouldn't, come back to bite you in the ass for a while. I'm not saying 'ever' but definitely a 'while'. Well, my ass was starting to get tired of all the depressing bite marks from this situation. My hurt feelings and my sore ass prompted me to plow through my house with a shopping bag and start dumping everything of his or that reminded me of him into the bottomless bag. The fluffy socks, t-shirts, photos, candles, CD's, a huge picture I was painting of the mountain top sunset, and, lastly, the earrings. Everything went in the bag. A bag full of memories, a bag full of hope, a bag full of hurt. *Oh, the drama!*

Ah, but that wasn't it. I wasn't quite past the 'can of worms' analogy of a relationship that I thought was a little more special than slimy bugs. I sat myself down at the dining room table with some paper and I started writing. Break #3 wasn't getting a poem this time but, to me, it might have been a more meaningful work of art on my part. Here went my closure. I can't relay what I wrote for two reasons. 1. It's private (for him) and 2. I can't remember all the details except for one, which I'll share.

I AM NOT A CAN OF WORMS. EVER. Ewww.

I explained my disappointment and disgust of his analogy and decided to refer to myself as a Can of Flowers instead. *Yes, flowers.* Flowers grow from a little seed. Flowers bloom when they are taken care of properly. Flowers represent beauty and life. I was no worm nor would I ever be one. As far as I was concerned, there was only one worm in this situation and since I was already the flower, it couldn't have been *me*. I continued on, wishing him happiness with whomever or whatever allows him that and I signed off. A lot of words, a lot of feelings, and a lot of disappointment that had never been truly shared up until now. Our ship went down a long time ago and I was taking the lifeboat out of there! He could do the drowning this time because I was suddenly feeling a whole lot of air filling up my lungs where I felt the need to inhale deeply and blow it all out.

The exhale sent my lifeboat into the safety of Thelma's arms, where she took the letter and the bag of memories and, so sweetly, dropped it at his door for me. I might have been feeling a bunch of muscle around *my* house, but there was no way in hell I was going to chance running into him on *his* own doorstep. I might have been a chicken but I was no fool! So Thelma came through for me again. First it was the Christmas present, now it was the break-up. I guess you have to know who to turn to in certain situations!

Notes to self:
New Year *does not* always mean New Start.
Worms are *ugly*! Be a flower.

Contestant # 7

losure. I'd like to think that I had closure and finality with Break #3, but I knew I probably never would. Unfortunately, he made too much of an impact on my life and I could only hope to learn to appreciate it over time and *pretend* in my *head* that I had my closure. At any rate, it was my closure. I gave it to myself and I needed to learn to live with it. Closure sucks but it's an important concept to keep in mind in order to play tricks with your head and emotions. Funny, I went from playing head games with Break #3 to playing head games with myself. I don't know what's worse, over analyzing Break #3 or trying to fool my brain on a daily basis that I was good and over it. Head games….can't live with 'em, can't live without 'em….so I played them with myself because I was missing him.

Maybe I needed a therapist again. *Yes! I went to a therapist. Doesn't everybody at some point?* I needed an unbiased opinion and psychoanalysis of whatever messes I kept creating for myself. My therapist really was a wonderful old gal and I became quite attached to our $175 weekly sessions of me sitting on her couch reaching for tissues. It was so textbook-therapist but she broke up with me after a while, too. *Yeah, that's right, she dumped me.* She said I was doing fine, that I knew what I wanted, and where I was headed. She said her door would always be open to me if I needed her. Here I thought I was going completely nuts and not making any progress at all. Either I was making progress or I was boring her to death and she couldn't take it anymore. I guess I was supposed to take getting dumped as a good sign that my head was twisted on straight for the time being. I wondered if it was twisted on correctly at *that* point? I wonder if she would've taken me back, and thought I was a dumb ass all along when I rambled off my New Year possibilities.

I decided not to rebound to my therapist for fear of sounding redundant on her couch and maybe *actually* boring her to death. Or, maybe even sounding foolish or ashamed. Instead, I logged into my old relationship to see what was cooking over the romantic internet. It had been a while but, like last time, my photo popped right up and smirked at me like I *was* a dumb ass. I wonder if my therapist would take me back if she knew I was flipping off my computer screen. That sounded twisted enough for therapy.

So, to pump up my ego a little, there were quite a number of hits on my profile which took a long time to sift through. When I sifted, I looked at the photos that have either emailed me or sent me winks. If there was someone staring at me that looked scary or unattractive (to me), I "x'ed" them out. My feelings hadn't changed about feeling the chemistry so I just wanted sift through and find something remotely close to chemistry.

I came across a couple of more that seemed nice enough and one, in particular, started emailing regularly. He typed really well and he clearly liked to chat online. He was a dark haired man from Danbury and he seemed really outgoing and humorous through his writing. I liked that, and anyone that could make me giggle by myself while staring at a computer screen earned some points. This guy was starting to sound like Contestant #7 on this merry-go-round shame show, I mean, *game show!*

Contestant #7 and I spoke on the phone a couple of times and he *was* very outgoing as I formerly suspected. He had a lot to talk about and was equally interested in me and what my life presently entailed. Although he was awfully chatty, I thought, for a split second, that he was showing signs of ADD, probably because of the mere fact that he couldn't seem to stay focused on any topic for more than 30 seconds at a time and then he would bring it up again 3 minutes later anyway. But for the moment, I just chalked it up to uncontrollable excitement. Head games with myself and I was surely just imagining it.

Contestant #7 and I decided to meet in Danbury on a Friday night. Normally, a girl should really have the guy come towards her area, but I really didn't mind driving, *plus-* it keeps me out of my hometown area *and* gives me a traveling reason to bolt, if necessary. These were two issues that kept popping up in the world of blind dating. I took my 30 minute drive and met him at a fun restaurant off the highway.

It was very busy, with no parking, so I 4-wheeled myself onto the shoulder of the road and climbed the hill to the place. Nothing like climbing a pavement hill in heels and feeling winded upon arrival. I wanted to continue my pant in order to catch my breath, but then I decided that wouldn't be too lady-like however, I was parched!

I spotted him right away because luckily he looked just like his half inch internet picture. He was waiting for me in the busy lobby with about 50 other people waiting for tables. I didn't really want to suggest switching venues since I wasn't too familiar with the area, so we went straight to the bar and ordered a drink. Luckily, we found a little real estate at the bar with a couple of stools. People were everywhere, leaning over us, yelling and laughing loudly. Not the most conducive environment to get to know someone but I was more thankful that I didn't end up in a back corner table again.

As we got comfortable on our bar stools, I started noticing brief, whimsical signs of the ADD I thought I had noticed before and I was surely not imagining it this time. Contestant #7 couldn't seem to get comfortable, wriggling his butt around, yanking at his clothes, and running his fingers through his hair. I don't want to be misunderstood, he was extremely friendly, very chatty, and found humor in everything but I couldn't quite figure out if he was nervous or just plain fidgety. We ordered a simple beer to start us off and see how it felt. We had no intention of sitting at a table, which was a relief to me considering the architectural table blueprints with Contestant #6.

So as I mentioned, the place was boisterous and hopping with people all around us. We began to chat safely about how we looked like our profile photos, and elaborating on some of our profile points. We talked about previous, disastrous dates, family, and work and, all along, I noticed his constant hand motion heading towards the area between his nose and upper lip. He was *picking* at something. *Oh God. What was he picking at?* I tried adamantly to ignore what I suspected, keeping the conversation going aimlessly. More picking. *Jesus! What was he picking at?* As he continued this strange picking ritual with his left hand, his right hand was simultaneously running his fingers through his hair, over and over and over again. *Holy crap, maybe this was actually Tourette's Syndrome!* Anyway, my beer started to go down a lot quicker than it was ten minutes ago. I think maybe it was my cricket calling, saying 'Get the hell outta here!'

Of course, when you want another drink at a bar, the bartender is usually nowhere to be found, but when you don't, there's a new drink sitting right in front of you. Since I was never one to turn down a free cocktail, I took the new one with grace and started sipping away.

As time was strangely passing, he kept on talking, occasionally turning to me as he said something. I found it difficult to focus on anything he was saying because I was becoming slightly obsessed with whatever he was obsessed with. I tried to get a glimpse of whatever action was happening above his lip, but he was discreetly keeping his hand around the area. *Mysterious, I must say.* Finally, his hand pulled away and I saw that it must have been a shaving knick in a precarious spot that he became mildly obsessed with. He got it. I knew this because now there was a drop of blood clinging for life on his upper lip. Did the hair styling stop? No. The hair never stopped, the wriggling never stopped, and the picking finally stopped only to reveal blood. I have to say, I was being a tremendously good sport about not wanting him to feel uncomfortable, so I decided to let my guard down a little.

I felt kind of bad for the guy because, obviously this was making him feel very self-conscience. I started getting funnier and returning to my witty old self as only my closest family and friends know about me. Contestant #7 caught on too, and, to my most shocking surprise, burst out in a cackle that was a cross between a hyena and woodpecker. It was the highest sounding shriek with a jabbing motion of a woodpecker stabbing at a poor tree. I was the poor tree in this ridiculous situation. So now I had wriggling, styling, picking, and cackling. *What else, do I dare to ask?*

"Want to order some appy's?" he asked.

"Appy's?" I asked back.

"Yeah, appy's. Let's get a little food here at the bar, I'm starving!"
Appy's?

"Sure we, can order something if you want", I replied. I really didn't want *appy's*. So far, I wasn't too thrilled about watching his hands in action, so I couldn't think of anything I wanted to do less than share finger food with him. I wish I could have just said no to the appy's but

I felt like he was having a rough start out of the gate, and I didn't want to be mean.

As the second drink wore on, he searched out the bartender to order those appy's, but, thankfully, the bartender was very busy to tend to us at that moment. We continued talking in the meantime and he continued to burst out in his awful cackle that was stopping other conversations around us. It sounded like the more comfortable he became, the more creatures I heard in his laugh. Now, there was a hint of excitable monkey mixed in with hyena and woodpecker. It was deafening but it was delivered with the most sincere smile and twinkly eyes, which made it very hard not to just smile along with his machine gun of a laugh.

"I wish we went someplace a little less busy", he said.

"That's okay", I replied "I like busy, fun places like this", I added.

"I know what you mean, but it's hard to get to know someone in such a noisy place", he mildly complained. He then suggested, "Maybe next time I can take you out for a nice quiet dinner someplace".

"That would be nice", I lied. All I could imagine was that high pitch cackle in a quiet little restaurant. After trying to accustom myself to this type of laugh I'd never heard, I thankfully started to forget about the earlier picking episode, however, his hair was never quite right because his continuous styling never stopped. I was starting to near the end of my second beer and I definitely didn't want another, knowing I had a 30 minute drive ahead of me -soon- so I sipped the remainder slowly.

It was at that magical moment that I swore I heard Bon Jovi singing out of my purse. I leaned down toward the corner of the barstool where my purse hung and, yes, I did hear my Bon Jovi ring tone! I quickly grabbed at my purse, reaching and shuffling inside for my phone to see who my spontaneous, unplanned hero was for saving me from this date. It was my mom. Now, normally I would complain here and there that she calls me too much, but this call was a pure welcome and smacked with good timing.

"Hello?" I answered.

"Oh, okay. Are you sure? Is she sure? Okay. I'll be home in about a half hour so just tell her to hang in there. Bye."

My daughter wanted to go home. She had no intention of sleeping over at my parents with my other daughter at a friend's house for a sleepover. She just wanted to come home. Had the date taken a different direction, I would have had my mom put her on the phone for a quick, motivational pep talk, but I didn't think that was necessary. In fact, it was a damn miracle as far as I was concerned. *Mommy's on her way!!!*

Contestant #7 looked at me sadly and, I must admit, I felt terrible. The truthful excuse that I was about to give him sounded like a total crock of shit.

"I have to run", I said, trying to seem a little disappointed.

"Why? What happened? Is everything okay?" he asked.

"Yeah, actually everything's fine but my daughter wants to just come home. She won't go to sleep at my parents and is a minute away from pitching a fit".

"That's too bad", he replied. "Can I take you out for that quieter dinner soon, though?" he asked me.

"Sure, we'll talk soon", I said. "And, thank you for tonight, it was great meeting you", I continued.

He stood up alongside of me and helped me with my coat. He kissed me on the cheek lightly and said goodbye. What a nice guy, what a strange guy, what an awful cackle. I wondered if there was a dot of blood on my cheek. I couldn't do it. Contestant #7 was over (*thank you, mom*).

Notes to self:
The only picking a guy should do…. is picking up the tab.
Cackling *cannot* do a "quiet" dinner.

Contestant #8

It took me quite a while to recuperate from that cackling disaster of a date. Looking back, I felt pretty awful that I couldn't give this guy another chance. I mean, after all, he was very kind and attentive. So what's a girl to do? It's not like we had instantaneous chemistry and I had to have him. Then, maybe, I would have tried to put the cackling aside (with some ear plugs). It just wasn't there and when it's not there, it's just not there!

Contestant #7 was one of the tougher email break ups that I had to endure. It's an online task that takes some guts and it's not a very rewarding accomplishment. It sure is a big step for online dating. At least, I felt that it was a big step because, I believe, the way in which one chooses to break up online separates the men from the dogs, or, in my case, the ladies from the tramps. *Hmmm, sounds like a movie I once saw.* Anyway, I was not a tramp, at least not until I met Contestant #8, but I'll get to that in a bit.

So I logged on to my square-shaped computer screen boyfriend, the internet, and clicked into the website that had become more of my daily companion than anyone else. I immediately located cackle-picker, and had a twinge of remorse for what I was about to do. I took a deep breath, and typed like a lady. Of course, I made no mention of his weird idiosyncrasies, ticks, wriggles, and picks. I just simply said that I thought we hadn't had much in common, after all. I also told him that it was wonderful meeting him and that I had a very nice evening. Lastly, I apologized for having to cut the date short and, finally, wished him the best of luck in his quest for Ms. Right. I thought that was pretty lady-like and I felt pretty good about clicking on the "send" button.

I guess Contestant Cackle was okay with it because he responded with a safe, somewhat lame, "good luck to you, too". I hated doing that.

At that point of my internet dating lifestyle, I was finding the post-date break up worse than the actual, blind meeting. *More growth?*

Again, there I was staring at a million faces, wondering what their story was, how much of their profile was truthful, and if I was completely wasting my time. I checked into my own profile and was surprised enough to see a message waiting for my response. I opened the email, read a very charming sentence or two, and I was mildly hooked. Who was this guy? I clicked on the picture attached to his email and, holy crap, the guy was hot! He was from the city and he was way too hot to be emailing some single mom in the burbs. I was wondering what the catch was but I was too intrigued not to respond. I sent him a very simple message back, trying to encourage a little more conversation so I could try to get a read on this guy. Well, it didn't take long because, clearly, this is what he does all day at work, OR this is what he does for work all day. I wasn't sure yet.

It didn't take long for this hot, city guy to get graphic. I don't think I had ever received any messages like that in my life. I hope I've made it clear that I am definitely not an uptight prude (although some of the recent situations might be questionable), but I couldn't believe what this guy was writing to me. I knew I should be reporting him to the Internet Dating Police, but for some sick reason, I kept egging him on because I just couldn't believe anyone would dare to type the things he was typing and send them to a perfect stranger. He talked about things he wanted to do to me in bed and in other locations with explicit descriptions and positions. He mentioned how great my lips were and wanted to know what they could do for him and if they could handle his size. He wanted me to jump on a train that afternoon and come straight to his apartment, and was suggesting what I should wear underneath my clothes, which was basically nothing. I could feel myself blushing and I was really trying to be very non-chalant about his forwardness. I think that's what was probably continuing to encourage him on the whole time. Maybe I should have called his bluff, taken his address, and hopped on a train, but not before taking off all my make-up and throwing on sweats! *What a hot weirdo.*

The details of that kind of weirdness can't even be typed, for fear of my parents getting the wrong idea. I would *hate* for them to think that I was *enjoying* that kind of attention or would *even* partake in that kind of trash. But I was. It's not like I had never had phone sex or sexting sessions but that was always with someone I knew or was in a relationship with. I think I was really getting a kick out of it for a few minutes because I *didn't* know this guy, but it really took me off guard. I really started mentally questioning the security of this type of website. There are sickos out there, floating around in cyberspace and some can look really hot! However, how does one have such enormous confidence and even bigger balls to carry on in that manner? I guess you can develop quite a set behind the one-way view of a computer screen. I mean, I *was* encouraging it for a bit there, too....

I eventually stopped contact from him and I "blocked" him. This was a perfect opportunity for me to test out the 'blocking' option on this website and see if it really prevented the twisted souls from penetrating my profile. *Penetrating*, being the key word with this guy, since that's apparently all he wanted to do to me. There is a blocking option on this website for people that are bugging you, harassing you, not taking no for an answer, and, I guess, people that sex message you. *Blocked! It worked.*

I took a cold shower (in my head), and continued my search for the potential Contestant # 8. Weird, sex message guy didn't warrant the title of Contestant #8 because his approach was way too New Millennium for me. Single moms from the burbs who are fairly new to the dating world can't possibly fall into a situation like that comfortably. Well, maybe some could, but I definitely couldn't. Ladies and Tramps.

So finally, I got an interesting email from a nice looking guy in Connecticut. He was a blonde, blue-eyed, witty guy who started off with "Let's cut to the chase. What's your number?"

I thought, 'here we go again'; however, I was equally intrigued! I liked that whole 'let's cut to the chase' kind of action. What I needed to figure out was whether this guy just didn't have the patience for all the small-talk-email-bullshit which I was tiring of myself lately. It felt kind of refreshing! Or, maybe my moon was strong or the stars were sexually lined up for me to have two of these whackos in a row! Anyway, I did my best to encourage just a smidgen more conversation through emails so that I didn't succumb to the immediate phone call. Sex message guy had left me a little wary so I wanted to watch myself this time. We managed to email a little more and his emails were funny, dry, and witty which is an ace in the hole for me. I loved it and I was on! I was finally conversing with someone who got my humor and who was able to respond with equal wittiness!

It didn't take long for us to move into phone conversations because it seemed the natural step to take after reading and responding to such fun emails. The phone conversations went well, but I had noticed that Contestant #8 didn't really like to touch upon anything too serious. In past conversations with other Contestants, phone talks were usually filled with divorce stories, kids, online experiences, and blah- blah catch up to begin to get to know each other. Not this guy. He didn't show too much interest in my past stuff but still had seemed very interested in getting to know my present stuff so we decided to meet.

We lived a little far from each other so we decided to meet in Greenwich, Connecticut at a place he was familiar with. I hadn't been to the area in a long time, so he gave me perfect directions and we planned to meet on a Friday night. While getting ready for my date, I was feeling a tiny bit nervous. I wasn't sure why, considering I had felt I was getting the hang of this blind date thing after all this time. However, I was feeling a little antsy about this one. I dressed safely in jeans, a black, fitted sweater, and black, heeled boots. My hair and make-up looked the same as it always did when I went out, so nothing out of the ordinary there. I left the house and was on my way. I was making good time until I hit Interstate 95, where there was huge traffic on a Friday evening, and, honestly, I started to get nervous again. This new guy seemed so much about the here and now, that I was worried about being late. I actually wondered if this guy had the patience to even wait for me even though I was honestly stuck in traffic. I looked at the number he gave me in case of any last minute changes, and pressed the numbers into my cell phone. He answered happily and made the psychic conclusion that I was stuck in the same traffic he was stuck in on the other side of 95. *Oh good.*

We still ended up meeting at about the same time, thanks to the equally annoying traffic. He beat me by a beer order which was comforting, because I don't like to be the first one to arrive and sit at the bar, waiting by myself. It's like an underlying fear that the date might actually choose not to show up, or see me first and turn quickly to the door before I see them. Kind of like what I had felt like doing in some of the dates in my recent past. Thankfully, he was there, with some real estate at the bar, and a nice tall beer. He had been looking towards the door for me, expecting me, so when I walked in, he stood up gentlemanly and gave me a grin and a wave. He had a seat saved for me, took my coat, and asked me what I'd like to drink. I kept it simple and had a beer too. Contestant #8 was good-looking and was similar to his picture. He wasn't quite as young as his profile photo had displayed, however, he was aging quite well, considering. He seemed a little heavier in his face and his hairline was a little more receded than his photo, but I was okay with it because he had an overall nice face and a solid presence, which I'm a total sucker for.

We joked a bit about things from previous phone conversations and finally told other online dating stories, making each other laugh. We were both receiving check-up texts from friends to see if the date was going well or not, so we laughed about that too, I guess because the date *was* going all right so far. We had a number of beers, and all the while, our body language was changing for the better. Instead of sitting straight on at the bar, our bodies began to turn and knees and arms were touching. We continued to have a great time together, and as we talked, our heads began to lean into each other. *That was a positive sign, I thought.*

"Usually I don't suggest food on the first meeting because it adds a bit of pressure to things", he stated.

I wasn't sure where he was going with this so I just raised my eyebrows with a grin, showing that I was waiting for him to finish his unfinished thought, or at least, explain.

"Okay, I'm starving. Let's get something to eat here at the bar. Are you cool with that, or does that create unwanted pressure?" he continued.

"I don't feel any pressure", I said "ask the guy for a menu", I added.

I figured, as long as this guy wasn't ordering *appy's*, I was fine with whatever! In fact, I decided to tell him that little snippet of a story and he almost fell off his stool in a combination of surprise and laughter! Then, of course, he busted my chops about it for the rest of our simple dining experience. *Ha ha.* Actually, I was glad for the idea of a little food so I could balance out the beer and gear up for the drive home.

At that moment, I decided to order a club soda with whatever food was coming. I was hoping the club soda would kill a little bit of my buzz because this guy was getting cuter and cuter by the second and the chemistry between us was on fire! Chemistry, *FINALLY!* It's taken 8 dates off this thing to find one evening of decent chemistry. *Was chemistry so hard to come by these days? Did chemistry only come with funny goggles and a lab coat? I was* feeling a little chemistry so I ran with it, as if I were stealing a lollipop from a kid on the sidewalk. *Mine!! Run!!*

After we ate *a little something* (that's what *I* call it, not appy's), he eyed my club soda with a little disdain.

"Why'd you switch over to soda?" he asked.

"I dunno. I think my buzz is getting the best of me and I still need to drive home", I replied.

"Are you planning on leaving very soon?" he asked, mockingly, with a raise of his eyebrows.

"Not sure yet", I replied evasively. Then, quiet. *Was I okay with this?* There was really only one person that I've been with in my lifetime where a comfortable silence was really okay. I didn't know this guy one bit so I wasn't sure if the silence was comfortable or just dead.

"Why are you looking at me like that?" I asked, suddenly feeling a little shy.

"What?" I prodded.

Looking down to his half drunk beer, he replied "nothing." Then the eyes crept back up to peer at me again, except they were accompanied by a playful grin. Bravely, yet unexpectedly, words came flying out of my mouth.

"You wanna kiss me, don't you?" *Oh my God! I couldn't believe I had just let that slip out of my lips. What was I thinking! Was I thinking?* He hesitated on the response. *Crap.* At that moment, as I began to lower my eyes in shame, Contestant #8 leaned in and kissed me like a movie star. *Nice! Now that was chemistry!*

The trick at that moment, was making it stop, coming up for air, remembering that we were still sitting at a busy bar with people all around. I'm pretty sure I didn't care. Kissing chemistry, that's all I cared about for the rest of the evening.

So I received another check-up text from Louise, wondering why she hadn't heard from me yet. According to my track record, I should have already been home with my own glass of wine, shooting the shit with her, licking my dating war wounds. Alas! I was not home yet and had no intention of going home yet. I texted her back, telling her everything was all good and I would call her in the morning. I'm sure her last thoughts were about where I was planning to sleep that night! In fact, I might have been wondering that same question a couple of short, fleeting moments here and there. *Would I remain a Lady or become a Tramp?* Uh, the pressure.

I decided to just go with the flow for the time being since everything was flowing smoothly but, eventually, the time did arrive to make some sort of move. We couldn't very well sit at a busy bar making out like the world was about to end. I mean, aren't those the people that get made fun of all the time? The ones with their tongues entwined, necks twisted, slobbering all over each other? I think those *are* the people that get made fun of, or maybe it's just my friends and I that make endless jokes about them, waiting for them to come up for air only to spot the disgusted smirks all over our faces. The looks on our faces that are screaming "GETTA ROOM!!!" No, I couldn't be on the receiving end of that any day with anyone. Definitely not a single mom of two young girls should be on the receiving end of that judgmental look. Of course, I don't slobber, so that was something to feel secure about.

"I think I should head out. I really can't drink anymore and get home safely and I'm thinking our conversation has taken a more intimate turn for this place", I said somewhat embarrassingly.

"You're probably right, I think we have the same distance to drive anyway. Let me grab the check", Contestant #8 replied.

Good, I was glad he wasn't giving me a hard time, although I quickly wondered *why* he wasn't giving me a hard time. *Was he not that into me? Could he take it or leave it? Was he giving in because he was probably not going to get laid?* Women are too damn analytical for their own good. I forced myself to shut up inside my head, let him pay the bill, and continue going with the flow to see where we floated.

He led me through the crowd, holding my hand as I followed close behind him to the door. Very gentlemanly! It turned out that we were parked in the same municipal lot across the street and, coincidentally, quite private and empty. Contestant #8 walked me to my car and even got in and started it up for me on that cold March night. We stood against my car, figuring out easy ways to stay warm. He was a great kisser, although he complimented me first on my appreciation for the art form of kissing. During one of our air breaks, I decided to make a move toward the car door because I was feeling a little silly making out in a parking lot like a teenager hiding from her parents. My motion toward the car was not necessarily an invitation for him to jump in the passenger seat; however that's how he perceived it. At least we were in a warmer climate. We hung out in my car for a little while and I seriously worried that if we continued this car business, I was going to become that Tramp, in a Greenwich, Connecticut parking lot. *Classy.*

Finally, we pulled ourselves away from each other long enough to say goodbye, and he told me he would call me in a couple of days. Right. *We'll see.*

He *did* call me a couple of days later, and not only that, he was sending me text messages throughout the days all week. This really got my blood pumping and I was starting to get a little jazzed up about this Contestant #8. We met again the following weekend, back in Greenwich which was definitely our half way point from each other. This time, he told me to meet him at a cool Tapas restaurant up the street from our original date. He beat me there and was waiting for me at the bar, looking toward the door for my arrival. *Jazzed.* He took my coat and sat me down, ordered me a drink and reminded me to relax. I guess I was feeling a little wound up and rushed. I needed to sit for a moment and decompress.

We basically picked up where we left off seven days beforehand and our only saving grace was that the hostess informed us that our table was ready. We sat across from each other in this very crowded place. The tables of two were so close that I was afraid my hips were going to jostle the couple's drinks at the next door table as I moved to the inside. Shuffling in sideways is not very graceful but if you turn your ass toward your empty table, it beats bumping their table around with your wide caboose.

Getting myself comfortable and situated with my surroundings, I took a peak at the most unfamiliar menu I've ever seen. *What the hell was all this?* I hadn't a clue and I think my face turned a little transparent with that notion. Contestant #8 asked me what I liked, firing off examples to me and all I had to do was say yes or no or I don't know. He was, again the gentleman, and ordered for the both of us. The guy liked to eat, that was for sure.

So now that we were in a more quiet setting for conversation, we were able to talk about whatever we wanted to. We couldn't get distracted with kissing because we were sitting across from each other and that would have been a little tricky. He told me about how he used to play in a band and all the gigs and costumes that he missed. I talked about my job and my friends. Funny, he didn't ask me too much about myself. In fact, he did most of the talking but that was okay because I was engaged and interested which I haven't been on a date in eons. I had been thinking about the band thing and that's always a little sexy for a girl, however, I couldn't recall if he told me what his current job was. I think I would have remembered, but I couldn't.

"Did you already tell me what you do now for a living 'cause I don't think you did", I inquired.

"No, I haven't because it never really comes out sounding very glamorous", he said.

"Well", I prodded, "spill".

Taking a deeper breath than normal Contestant #8 said "I drive a truck".

"A truck?" I asked as though not hearing him clearly the first time. I was fine with it but what kind of truck? A dump truck, a garbage truck, a tow truck, a what truck?

"I drive an oil truck and I deliver to gas stations all day", he informed me.

"Oh", I said. "Do you like it?" I continued.

"Yeah, it's a good, stable, consistent salary that the band couldn't offer me. So, yeah, it's okay. I make a ton of money and I'm home early everyday. I have to get up really early, but I've gotten used to that".

Wow, I was on my first trucker date. That would go over well with my parents. I would have to hash this out with a few of my friends first and see how it goes with them. I don't see why anyone should care. He was very nice, well-mannered, and gentlemanly. Who cared if he drove an oil truck everyday! *Hmmm, a trucker! Go figure!*

So after a lot of mental hemming and hawing, I decided that this would be a perfect opportunity to practice keeping my options opened. I didn't mean to be thinking in a snobbish way or a judgmental way, but coming from the affluent town that I grew up in, most people expect a person to date someone making a certain amount of money in a profession that allows plenty of time for networking, schmoozing, and golf. I don't exactly feel that way but some places are just the way they are. I was always a fan of the "click". When people click, then they click and there's not a damn thing anyone can do or say about it. I felt a click. Besides, I thought, maybe this guy does plenty of that other stuff *and* drives an oil truck! I liked him and I was going to date a trucker!

A couple of weeks had passed and it was chock- filled with calls and text messages, so at least the truck was still rolling. On came St. Patrick's Day, where I frolicked in the city with my friend and many firefighters, celebrating their success in one of their many parades. The day went straight into night and, after many a beer, it was time to hit the trains. As I was riding home, quietly reflecting my extremely fun-filled day, Contestant #8 sent me a text, requesting me to hop on the train to his town, deep into Connecticut.

"2 late" I sadly replied, "alrdy on way home".

Wow! How cool that he was thinking about me and wanted me to come over to him. That jazzed me up even more throughout the week and I was looking forward to the upcoming Friday which would be my next, sure possibility of seeing him again.

Around Wednesday, we spoke, and I mentioned the fact that I would be free in a couple of days. That should have been it, right? *Wrong.* Instead, I get this lame response about possible plans he might already have. This guy knew I had Friday nights free and that it was a pretty sure thing to hook up with me and make some plans. *Wrong, again.* He remained persistent about "possible plans" he might already have and he wasn't giving me any more information than that. Okay, a little hard- to-get game. It's been a while, but I bit the bait and tried to stay aloof and mysterious myself.

"I'll call you if anything changes for Friday, okay?" he said.

"Okay, no problem", I replied. Hmmm, he wasn't going to call. I guess I just figured with all the hot chemistry the last couple of nights we hung out, it shouldn't be that difficult to commit to another date! *Wrong, yet again!*

The next day I checked into all my online boyfriends on the website and noticed a few more winks and a couple of messages. I clicked on the messages and there was Contestant #8, staring at me with his pompous smile, luring me into reading his freshly typed message. Why the online message after all our phone communication? I decided that was a bit cowardly before I even read it.

I read:

"Hey Jacey, I've had a really fun time hanging out with you but I have also met someone else and I think I want to see where it goes. Take care".

What!!?? Was he kidding? I had felt like I just got slapped in the face. Did he not remember last weekend when we were steaming up the windows, while he was begging me to come home with him? Uh - *FLAG*....I didn't go home with him. That's all he wanted. I was wined and dined for the first time in so long, only for him to fulfill his hopes of getting laid. Well, I was feeling a little pissy, so I typed back and let some words fly on him. I can't remember exactly what I wrote, but I'm sure it had the ring of "you mother fucker trucker!" Oh, and "good luck in your search". Contestant #8 was over.

Notes to self:
Keep an open mind, but, be wary of the wine and dine.
Truckers can be as slick as the oil they deliver!

Contestant #9

I have to say, I was a little disappointed about the Contestant Trucker. Actually, I was a lot disappointed. I had been waiting so long to feel any smidgen of online spark so I guess I got my hopes up just a tad too much. Being hopeful online didn't seem far different from being hopeful offline. It still hurt when the slightest rejection crept in. I guess I was starting to realize how the other Contestants might have felt when I gently rejected them, assuming they were into me that much when their rejection crept in. Oh well, I had to get back to it and not let that mother fucker trucker discourage me too much. At least, he proved that there can be a spark of chemistry in the mysterious world of online dating, *and*, that I was still desirable enough to want to be slept with, even if it was intended to be a one night stand or a parking lot stand--whatever.

Later on in the month, my close friend wanted to catch up and get together for a bit. I hadn't seen in her in a while, and I wanted to hang out as well. She, being one of my oldest friends, had always thought to include me in any fun thing she knows of. She has always made me feel like I was the first person she put a call into, to let me know of any upcoming plans. She was the phone call that lured me into the city the night I met my Scottish angel.

After touching base, we decided we were going to meet at a local street fair up north, closer to where she lives. In a cute town called Fishkill, they closed the streets, had live music, tents of food, and open pub doors to the public. I explained to her that I had been in touch with, what seemed like a really nice guy, from the dating website. I also told her that I might consider meeting up with him for a drink after the street fair because he lived in her neck of the woods. It just seemed easier to kill two birds with one stone since it wasn't around the corner from me and since my friend was really easy going like that. My friend was really fine with that, in fact, too fine. She loved hearing my dating stories and always released a hearty laugh after each one of my playbacks. I think *she* was more excited to meet one of my dates than *I* was.

I had been emailing with him and talking on the phone with him for a couple of weeks at this point so, technically, it was probably good timing to finally meet. I let him know that I was heading north to the street fair and that we would be going to a local pub after we walked through the fair for a bit. I suggested he could meet me at the pub and I asked him if he minded that I would be out with a friend already.

"No", he responded, dripping with friendliness. "Just gimme a call when you get to the pub and I'll come meet you".

"Okay", I said. That was easy.

My friend and I were strolling through the fair enjoying the people-watching festivities when my cell phone rang. I didn't recognize the number but then it dawned on me that it could be Contestant #9. I had called him from my cell a little while ago, so now he had my cell number. I decided to let it go to voicemail, just in case it wasn't him, and I called in for my new message a minute later.

"Hi Jacey, I'm at the street fair walking around looking for you. Where are you? Call me back and let me know where you are so I can come find you. My house is only right around the corner, so I decided to stop over and see if I could find you."

Huh.

Was that weird or was that cute? I hadn't made a decision yet. I mean, hadn't we just spoken a half hour ago and decided to meet at the pub later on? I started to explain all this to my friend when my cell phone rang again.

Same number.

Voicemail, please.

A minute later, I listened again.

"Hi Jacey, it's Contestant #9 again. Just wondering where you are. I am walking through the street fair and I can't find you. Do you look like your picture? Call me back and tell me where you are and what you're wearing so I can find you. Bye".

Huh.

Definitely not cute, but borderline weird. This time, I began rehashing the voicemails to my friend and she stood there staring at me with her lips curling up at the corners. She burst out laughing in her signature cackle that becomes extremely contagious. Her cackle comes deep from the soul, exiting with a hearty, sincere sound. No animal mating calls are etched into her laugh like Contestant #7! Still laughing, we entered a local pub for a quick brew to drink away the hysterics that were already brewing of the night ahead.

"Didn't you tell this guy we were gonna meet him later at the other pub?" she asked.

"Yeah, I did. I told him I hadn't seen you for a while, that we were gonna walk around a bit, then head to the pub where he could meet us for a drink".

I didn't think that sounded confusing, but, then again, I didn't know this guy from a hole in the wall, so who knew if he had a couple of screws loose in the comprehension section of his semi-stalker brain. Yeah, that's right, I had already nicknamed him "Street Fair Stalker". I would happily continue to call these guys Contestants, and will continue to do so IF they don't earn themselves a different title.

My phone rang *again!* This time, I decided to answer it, in case I wanted my frustration to be heard through my tone of voice, which I'm mildly famous for among all that know and love me.

"Hello?"

"Hi- Jacey?"

"Yes?"

"It's Street Fair Stalker, where are you? Are you still at the street fair? I've been calling you, have you gotten my messages? Do you wanna meet up 'cause I'm walking around here looking for you."

Holy shit.

"Hi. I'm still strolling with my friend at the street fair. I have gotten your messages but you haven't allowed me much time to call you back before the next message. I thought we planned to meet up at the pub later on", I clarified.

I think I answered all of his questions in order, but I was getting a little pissy already. Not only was he searching me out in a freakin' street fair, he now had my cell number to harass me with while he was searching.

Holy shit.

"Oh yeah, that's fine to meet later. Ya know, my house is right around here so I figured I would stop by the street fair, have a look around, and maybe find you."

"I understand", I responded "But I did have plans with my friend as well, so we're just gonna finish up around here and then hit the pub. She is meeting her boyfriend there anyway."

"Okay. No problem. I'll just head back to the house and wait for your call", he said.

"Cool", I replied. "Maybe like another hour and I'll give you a ring, okay?"

"Yeah, that's great. Gimme a ring when you're ready", he said.

We said a quick goodbye and I turned to my friend as the curls at the edges of her lips were really starting to crawl up her cheeks.

"Don't even!" I yelled at her with a belly laugh rising up through my gut. We laughed our asses off, her with her infamous cackle and me with my belly laughs that turn silent, as though I can't get any air in my lungs to make a laughing noise.

The hour passed as we stopped here and there for a draft beer being offered all along the street. We watched as families wandered about and teenagers mischievously tried to figure out how to cause some trouble without getting caught. Eventually, we decided we had exhausted all the street fair had to offer and headed back to the car.

"Gonna call your new boyfriend now?" my wise ass friend asked.

"Yeah, I guess I should. He might be very worried about me!" I replied with a smirk on my face.

I probably wasn't being very nice but it was really hard to deal with this situation in a serious manner. In fact, finding humor in something potentially uncomfortable is usually the path I tend to travel. It was a well-worn path in my life already and, after this dating phase of my life, the path should be paved!

We drove over to the pub, as planned and I called Contestant #9 when we got into our parking space. I figured this would allow me a few extra minutes to settle in with a cocktail before he arrived.

The place was getting crowded and, thankfully, I didn't know anyone except the friend I was with, considering this guy had already proven to be a mild fruitcake. My friend and I sat at the bar, chatting it up and people watching when a very clean cut guy walked through the front door. My radar was up and I had a feeling it was him. He walked in alone, looking around, which is usually a dead giveaway. I took a chance and raised my hand for a quick wave to see if he responded, and he did. He approached with a friendly smile and greeted me.

"Jacey?"

"*Street Fair Stalker.* How are you?" I responded.

"Good. Good. Did you guys have a nice time?" he asked.

"We did, thanks", I politely introduced him to my friend. One of the greatest qualities of this particular old friend of mine is that she can literally talk to anyone. She always has some sort of 6 degrees of separation with people and never forgets a face. That wasn't the case with Contestant #9; however she was a fantastic ice breaker for me!

"Do you want a drink?" I asked him.

"No thanks, I don't drink", he replied with a smile.

Huh. Don't drink? I don't know why, but that always sent a flag up for me. *Did someone not drink because they were previously an addict? Did someone not drink because they turned into a psychopath? Did someone not drink because they were a bag of nerves? Why does a young guy not want a drink?*

"Actually, I'll have an iced tea", he said, changing his beverage mind.

Iced tea? How about a water? O'Doul's? Or let's really shake things up…Long Island Iced Tea?

The place was getting busier and my friends boyfriend showed up to lighten the mood even more. He's a happy, go-lucky kind of guy who loves to laugh and talk. As far as Contestant #9 was concerned, it was a little hard getting to know more of him in that environment, with my friends around. I felt distracted and uninterested and maybe just not feeling the click. I remained polite and pleasant as my girlfriend excused herself to run to the ladies room.

Okay, now we had a few minutes alone, let's see where this was really headed. Contestant #9 moved a little closer to me, acting as though the loudness of the place was making it hard for him to hear me. Actually, I wasn't saying much which is why it was probably hard for him to hear me. It just wasn't clicking and he wasn't being funny or witty or interesting enough for me to even feel the slightest connection.

I stretched a little on the barstool. *Mistake*. He moved closer. I looked for my friend. Not back from the bathroom yet. *Crap*. He moved closer with the raise of his arm. My eyes darted around the room but I tried to keep a pleasant smile on my face that wasn't too inviting, although I think he already made his own invitation as his hand moved onto my shoulder. *What the hell....*

Contestant #9 began massaging my shoulder!

"You seem a little tense. Are you?" he asked me.

"No, I'm okay. Maybe I'll just get off this barstool and stand for a bit", I said.

"Here, let me rub you out a little", as he continued to massage with one hand all around my upper shoulder and into my neck. I really made every attempt to stand but he wasn't having it so I was feeling a little stuck and trapped. He wasn't being rough or hurtful, just downright weird. I didn't know this guy. There was no click. No chemistry. Nothing in common. No sharing of the beverage. So, really, there shouldn't be any massaging of any sort. My eyes kept darting around for my friend. *Where the hell was she? Was she restyling her hair or something?* Bad timing for her and for me. Apparently great timing for Contestant #9!

By now, he was quite close into my personal space, touching my personal shoulder and I was beginning to really take it personally. I'm all about the affectionate touch, or the whisper in the ear *if* it's mutual or invited, but it wasn't mutual or invited. This guy had gone from a Street Fair Stalker to a Creepy Bar Massager and I just wasn't sure what title he earned more! All I knew was that this date was over.

My friend finally returned and we made the eye contact decision to cut the evening short. She knew as well as I did that this guy was strange. My eyes became transparent and my walls grew higher. A guy can lean in and massage all he wants, but when the girl gets stiffer in the shoulders, it's time to hit the streets! Back to the fair, Freako! Contestant #9 was over.

Notes to Self:
Street Fairs are for good fun, not stalkers.
Massages are for spas, not bars.

Contestant #10

I was really beginning to think that this online dating was for, well, basically, anyone but me. I wasn't having any luck with any of the dates since I joined this ridiculous fad of meeting people. Certainly, there were chuckles to be had with my dating scenarios, but, somewhere in the depths of my head, I knew this was all crap. Clearly, it worked for some people. I mean, my neighbor met someone on the same website and was now happily married. I went to the wedding. The guy was very nice, very normal, and the ceremony itself was somewhat inspiring. Inspiring? Yeah, because it *can* happen and he was the living proof. Maybe not my living proof, but his new wife's. Also, someone from work was now engaged to her online date and planning her upcoming wedding. More proof. More inspiration. I wasn't willing to give up just yet. I may not have found Mr. Right, but the stories were getting funnier, or weirder, whatever the preference.

After letting Contestant #9 down gently, yet happily, through an email, I continued to check my own profile. So far, I wasn't having a communication dry spell. It seemed that when one door closed, another one opened. *Huh, reminds me of a song I know.* Anyway, there was Contestant #10 looking at me with gentle brown eyes. His picture wasn't great, considering a quarter of his head was chopped or cropped off. I hope that wasn't on purpose, like he was trying to hide something. We conversed for a few days and he was chatty and kind of cute. I enjoyed communicating with him and since I was on such a roll, I figured let's not waste a ton of time on the phone. Let's just meet.

He lived a little north of me but we new our halfway point immediately. A little town 10 minutes from me would be it. Growing up around here allows me the knowledge that this particular meeting town was all of 18 inches long. It's a very small town with not a whole lot of choices to meet one for a date. The places I knew of were simple, modern, and easy. The place Contestant #10 knew of was older than dirt.

"Why don't we meet at Tor-CHEE-a's?" he suggested.

"Torchias?" I corrected

"Isn't it pronounced 'Tor-CHEE-a's'?" he responded

"I think it's pronounced with an 'sh' sound- (Tor-sha's), not a 'ch'. It's Italian, not Mexican", I joked.

He laughed, too and I like a guy that can laugh at his own mistakes. Good sign.

We picked a Friday night to meet, and, unfortunately since this place had been around as long as I lived in the area, it wasn't considered much of a hot spot at all. The place was a bit run-down and dingy, with that real old-time tacky style. It looked like it had been unsuccessfully updated over the years but it really needed a gutting and make over, instead.

Contestant #10 was waiting for me outside at a little chair beside the front door as I pulled my car into the side lot. I walked around to the front, where he stood and he walked towards me, greeting me with a handshake and a peck on the cheek.

"Nice to meet you", he said to me.

"You too", I replied back. "Have you been waiting long?"

"Nah, just got here a few minutes ago. You look great!"

"Thanks", I said, somewhat looking down at him. Maybe I overlooked his height on his profile because I probably should have worn flats.

We entered the restaurant, which is exactly how I knew it would be. Wrought iron fixtures hanging from plaster walls with fake flower arrangements pouring out of them that could have used a little dusting. Mirrors everywhere, probably as a tactic to make the place look more spacious. Fake trees in every corner. Candle sconces scattered about in any open space of wall. Old carpeting that should have been ripped up but at least could have used a cleaning and table chairs that really belonged in a pizza parlor. I hated those chairs because they were the kind that felt wobbly beneath you and any normal woman's ass hung over the sides, making one feel like Large Marge ready to dig into a meal.

Again, I really would have preferred meeting for a drink rather than dinner. I'm just not partial to meeting for a meal on the first date but this wasn't the first time I had been sucked into this situation so I handled myself with grace and dignity. We sat at a table of two, against a wall, and opposite a wall of mirror. I glanced to the left and spotted my butt perched on the little Goldilocks chair meant for Baby Bear. *Whatever.*

Contestant #10 continued to be chatty and talked a lot about himself. That was really fine with me for the initial conversation because it allowed me a few minutes to see what he was all about. He talked about his 15 minutes of fame as a US Open ball boy back in the day. He talked about his avid tennis playing skills and how athletic he was. I'm sure he was, even though he didn't look very athletic. Maybe that wasn't nice, but after a while, I wasn't getting a word in edgewise so maybe I was starting to feel a little punchy. He kept coming back to his ball boy days and he exhausted that topic beyond belief. I thought it was very interesting, considering, I spent my entire childhood attending the US Open every year. My family grew up as avid tennis players too but I didn't have much opportunity to throw that into the conversation. Finally, I seized my moment and chimed in that my dad had been playing, like, forever.

"Your dad's a tennis player?" he asked inquisitively.

"Yeah, like his whole life. He still plays a coupla nights a week with his buddies and he's always involved in some sort of tournament", I said

"Really? Where does he play?" #10 asked.

"Well, he plays everywhere, but mostly right here in this town."

"I betchya I've played with him before!" he exclaimed excitedly.

"Ya think?" I asked "I mean, he is much older than you."

"What's his name? I'm sure I've played with him before!"

"Uh…" I hesitated, "Jeff Blah-Blah."

"Hmmm, don't recognize that name, but I'm positive we have played!"

Okay time to change the subject because clearly, this tennis thing was becoming a dead ball. The waitress came over and asked us if we would like a drink.

"I would *love* a drink", Contestant #10 stated.

Oh, thank God.

"I'll have a Sprite", he requested

Damn it!

"Uh, I'll have a seltzer", I said. *Damn it, again.*

We looked at the menu and we decided to eat 'light'. I was happy about that because of the "dinner thing". He looked all over the menu like 400 hundred times. Front to back, back to front, flipping the pages back and forth like it was a diner menu. *Light*, he said. How much is there to search for that's *light*, I wondered.

The waitress returned with our *sodas*.

"Hey, how do you pronounce the name of this place?" he asked the girl.

"It's Tor-CHEE-a's, right?"

The waitress responded politely, "Actually, it's Torchia's, with a 'sh' sound rather than a 'ch' sound."

I sat there with a twinkle in my eye because, obviously, this guy wasn't making light of my telephone correction and wanted to check it for himself. At least I was right.

"Are you ready to order?" she asked.

"Sure, we're gonna eat light. You go first", he said, looking at me.

She turned towards me and, if I didn't know any better, she might have raised her eyebrows slightly, acknowledging something that wasn't quite clear yet with this guy. A woman knows!

"I'll just have a small salad with vinaigrette and the stuffed mushroom appetizer as my meal".

I was good with that. Light. No muss, no fuss, and no lengthy four course meal with possible nipple pointing.

"I'll have a small salad, too, with ranch dressing. I'll also have an order of Chicken Fran-Says-See", he said.

What???

The waitress did everything in her power not to burst out laughing and I was still trying to comprehend what the hell he just renamed that old, Italian dish.

I couldn't believe my ears!

"Chicken Francese?" she repeated, correctly.

"Yeah, umm,hmm, Chicken Fran-Says-See", he restated the same as before.

Oh my God. First, Tor-CHEE-a's, then, Chicken Fran-Says-See??? Clearly, this guy didn't have an Italian bone in his body, that, or he didn't get out much. I can understand screwing up the name of the place if you're unfamiliar with it, but screwing up Chicken Francese? I have heard pronunciations like Fran-Chez, Fran-Sez, Fran-Chaze, Fran-Sayz. But never Fran-Says-See!! That's utterly ridiculous. This guy must have done very well with his phonics lessons back in elementary school, sounding out each, individual letter and sound! This moment was going to be a turning point for me on a very personal level.

As we waited for our meal, because I can't bear to type his phonetic awareness again, he continued to remain obsessed with tennis and the possibility of playing with my father at some point in his lifetime. I couldn't seem to change the subject for the life of me, so I hunkered down for what would be another strange and boring date.

I laughed when I was supposed to laugh, and was serious when I was supposed to be serious, and I was interested when I was supposed to be interested. I was really bored to tears....until the food arrived.

The waitress set down the salad plates, which was a plate of iceberg lettuce, a wedge of tomato, an olive, and drenched with dressing. I cut my salad up like I always do because I hate the idea of trying to shove large lettuce leaves in my mouth loaded with a drippy dressing. My date, on the other hand, had no intention of caring whether he shoved a whole lettuce leaf in his mouth or a whole head of lettuce in his mouth! I then watched him shift into, what seemed to be an "eating stance" that consisted of his right hand planted on his right thigh, his left hand holding his utensil from the top, and his whole upper body hunched over his plate like a caveman who had never had a more than a fish stabbed at the end of a spear before.

As I quietly pecked at my side salad, cut up into smaller, bite-sized pieces, Contestant #10 was hunched over his plate, eating salad like his ship was going down. Ranch dressing was splashing, red onions were swinging, tomatoes were squirting. Lettuce remains that didn't quite fit into his mouth were being cut by his front teeth, allowing them to drop back onto the plate, waiting for the next stab of his fork. As I was taking all this in, I realized the tennis talk finally ceased, probably because he was using his entire air intake to shove the salad down before the threat of someone came and took it away.

I glanced at him now and then, in awe, noticing that the only clear view I had of him was the top of his head, where 3 separate bald spots evenly placed, front and sides. I guess his bald spots had to be a better view then of him plowing through a plate of ranch soaked iceberg!

When he finally came up for air, I was about three quarters through with my salad. He was about to say something when I think he saw my transparent look of disgust spread across my face. Contestant #10 had ranch dressing dripping from his freakin' chin! *UH! Did I have the word IDIOT stamped across my forehead? Was that why I was attracting one idiot after another? Could I at least find a guy with manners? A napkin?*

He straightened up in time to receive his next, *light* course of…… Chicken Fran-Says-See!!! His eyes lit up like Christmas morning and he quickly resumed his eating stance. As he demolished and devoured his chicken, I quietly ate my 6 little mushrooms, praying this date would be over soon. He pretty much ate his main course the same way he ate his appetizer. If anyone had been watching him sawing into his chicken one-handed with the side of his fork, they'd think this guy had never been allowed to eat in public his whole life. The table shook fiercely every time he tore into his chicken and sauce spattered about him, as he slopped each bite in a pool of Fran-Says-See sauce before slurping it into his awaiting mouth. At the rate this guy was going, he was going to eat the plate and bread basket before I got to my 4th mushroom. Really, this date couldn't last too much longer.

Within the next few minutes, Contestant #10 did everything but lick his plate clean like a dog. I left a mushroom because, frankly, I completely lost my appetite.

"Would you like some dessert or coffee?" the waitress asked.

"I'm fine", I said, "Full." (of enough stomach turning for one night).

"How could you be full?" Contestant #10 asked.

"You barely ate that much", he pointed out.

"It was a *light* dinner", I remarked.

And, I didn't feel the need to eat my way through the walls of a fucking restaurant like a damn termite, I thought.

I took initiative.

"Maybe just the check?" I asked both of them.

"Oh, okay. I guess the check please", he agreed, thankfully.

He paid, with the first sign of gentlemanly manners all evening and we headed out the door. As far as I was concerned, that date lasted an hour and a half longer than it should have. In fact, I felt someone owed me that hour and a half back at some point in my lifetime. I still stand by my policy of grabbing a first date drink rather than a meal…if one can help it. This date was a perfect example of why.

"Do you like pool?" he asked, out of the blue.

"Like swimming or billiards?" I asked back for clarification.

"Shootin' pool. Billiards. Do you?"

"I guess. It's been a while. Maybe like 15 years. Why?" I asked idiotically, because apparently I *am* an idiot.

"Well, there's a great pool hall up where I live and thought it would be fun to go shoot some pool. You up for it?"

"Ummm, well, didn't we meet here because it was the halfway point?" I asked.

"Yeah, I guess you're right. Kind of a drive for you at this point, huh?"

"Yeah, it kind of is. Besides, I have to go relieve the babysitter because she has plans tonight, too and I told her I wouldn't be late."

"Okay. Well, we should definitely plan on doing this again. Would you be cool with that?" he asked, as if my answer would be none other than an 'absolutely, you hot, sexy thing'.

"Well, let's touch base next week and see what's up", I said cautiously.

I'll tell ya what's up….nothing, except your face out of your plate now. And…your time's up!

"Sounds good, Jacey, I'll call you next week. I had a really good time with you tonight."

"Me, too", I lied.

He walked me to my car, gave me a quick peck on the cheek which matched the one upon arrival, and I got in my car and left. Contestant #10 was over. We would not be going out again, however, as I mentioned, this moment in time was an integral turning point for me. *Huge personal growth was happening.*

Notes to Self:
Phonetic Awareness does not equal common sense.
Sloppy salad and slurpy Fran-Says-See is not sexy---EVER!

Contestant #11

D id I log off indefinitely? No. Did I find the love of my life? No. However, I might have just been so utterly inspired with an idea, that it made my head spin, swirling with recent recollections. I was going to write a book and Fran-Says-See man was my ultimate inspiration! But the idea would have to wait because I was still trying to find Mr. Right floating around in cyberspace.

At the risk of sounding redundant, I was more determined than ever to get my money's worth from this website. I had been bombing date after date with as much success as a fighter pilot aiming for his target. It seemed that the actual launch of the dates were getting easier but the landings were really sucking time and time again.

I tried to put the stalker and the sloppy eater out of my head and forge forward with a good attitude. Back on the website, I spent more time browsing and clicking a hello to any reasonable Tom, Dick, or Harry. I was getting the feeling that the pickings were getting slim and I couldn't possibly fathom the idea that I had gone on that many dates that now I had no one to choose from, because I hadn't!

I tried a couple of different zip codes so I could see some new, fresh faces. Maybe someone would bite and take a chance on the average girl. I checked into Manhattan first. After many clicks and reading, it had come to my surprising attention that the majority of men in the city wanted arm candy. Either they were serial daters, players, or claimed they 'lived life to the fullest', were 'optimists', or 'enjoyed everything life has to offer'. *That's crap!* These guys wanted nothing more than a size 2, bleach blonde, who they can take to parties and schmooze their way through the evening and into bed….with the arm candy. Okay, maybe that's a little harsh. Maybe not *all* guys in the city were like that. Maybe not *all* the profiles read like that (although, those catch phrases were getting a little played out). And, maybe not *all* arm candy girls hit it with their dates *all* the time. Maybe, the mere fact was, I was getting annoyed. I was getting annoyed, frustrated, and a little disappointed. *Wasn't I doing it? Wasn't I putting myself out there? Wasn't I doing what everyone suggested I do? Wasn't I dating, dammit!* I changed the zip code and decided to search New Jersey. Why? I have no idea but I figured, what the hell.... it's not *that* far.

Well, wouldn't you know, a very nice Jersey boy decided to contact me back. He was very, very nice looking and I'm usually biased about anyone from New Jersey, keeping Jon Bon Jovi at the highest level of good looking from New Jersey, well, anywhere. So Contestant #11 was a firefighter from New Jersey. It sounded yummy and I hadn't been out on a date with a firefighter yet which was definitely something on my personal to-do list. I figured since I was never going to go on a date with Jon Bon Jovi from New Jersey, I guess the firefighter was the next best thing!

We emailed a lot and he really did seem nice enough. We only spoke on the phone once and he really didn't talk that much. I concluded that maybe some guys are just shyer than others and this might be a perfect example. Or, he just wasn't a big talker. That's fine, because I can talk! In that same phone conversation, we had made our plans to meet. He was doing most of the distance driving and I felt a little badly about that, but I was relieved, too. He didn't seem to mind the idea and we decided to meet down by the Hudson River, right over the Tappan Zee Bridge - where I met sneaky-kisser-astrology guy many Contestants ago.

Contestant #11 and I met at a restaurant that had a decent bar crowd, okay food, and often, a band playing. I suppose it's a pretty ideal spot to meet a blind date. We met outside and he *was* cute! He was a tad bit short for my taste but I didn't care because he had blue eyes to die for! I might've possibly considered starting a little fire for the fireman to see his hotness in action!

We entered into the restaurant and found an empty cocktail table to roost at. At the time, it so happened I was trying out the Atkins diet, and therefore couldn't have my customary beer (carbs!) so I ordered a Gin and Tonic. I don't even know if that's on the Atkins menu but I figured it had to be better than beer! Contestant #11 ordered a beer which kind of goes in tow with my idea of a hot fireman! He and I chatted lightly over our drinks, although I was doing most of the talking. He was mostly looking at me with those penetrating blue eyes. I wasn't quite sure what to make of it but I knew he wasn't acting weird, pointing at my nipple, slurping salad, or cackling yet. So I kept talking.

Half way through his first beer, he politely excused himself to the men's room. *Okay. Not a very big bladder, I guess.* I sat and people watched until he returned. I thought maybe he would dream up a few more things to say while he was peeing but he had not. I pushed forward with whatever conversation I could conger up. I sipped my very strong Gin and Tonic, silently wishing for my sacred beer *(damn carbs!)*. Contestant #11 finished his beer after a little while and excused himself to the men's room again.

As I sat there mildly astonished with his small bladder, I began questioning if maybe he was doing drugs or something in the bathroom other than peeing. Nah! He was a fireman. Weren't they routinely drug tested or something? Besides, if this guy was doing drugs, I think I would have noticed. If he were stoned, his beautiful blue eyes would have been rimmed with red and he would have been spacey and giggly. No, he wasn't stoned. If he were wired, his beautiful blue eyes would have been popping out of their sockets and he would have been a non-stop talker. Clearly that wasn't the case. I decided to finish my drink and see what happened upon his return. He ordered two more drinks for us when he came back. I don't know, maybe he *did* have an ultra small bladder.

We resumed our cocktail spots at the small table where he proceeded to not talk some more. Now, I considered myself a friendly individual with a fairly outgoing personality. I can laugh at myself as well as others and I can certainly talk the paint off the walls in the right environment or with the right company. I was literally running out of things to talk about. I *never* run out of things to talk about. When I have a lull in conversation, there might be a break of silence or reflection. It may be a comfortable silence with the right person or it might be a slightly stressful silence with the wrong person. This was definitely the latter.

I sipped my drink a little faster and learned almost nothing about this man in a drink and a half's time. There he went again- to the men's room. *What the hell?* Maybe he was making calls to his friends or to his girlfriend or, dare I say, to his wife! *Holy crap! Did I miss the ring? Was he wearing a ring?* Is he one of those sneaky guys that takes off his ring and leaves it on the dashboard of his car when it's convenient for him? I had to get a better look if this guy ever returned from the bathroom. Maybe he snuck out the window. I was pretty sure that only happened in movies but with the strange dates I had been on, I wouldn't be surprised if it happened to me.

He returned.

"Sorry", he said.

"That's okay. Everything all right?" I asked.

No ring.

That was good, but still no excuse for the constant ditching to the bathroom.

"Yep", he replied.

That's it? That's it. I made a solid decision to ditch this drink and ditch this guy. It was definitely going nowhere except to the bathroom three times already. I was actually second guessing myself as a lush who can bang back her cocktails and never feel the need to pee. Actually, in a girls world, we choose 'not to break the seal' unless it's a dire circumstance. Once we pee, we pee all night and it's a real drag. If we can hold it, we can conquer a few hours in peace and without pee interruptions. This helps us not miss out on any funny laughs with our friend's, interesting people walking through the door, a favorite song blasting from the speakers, or the really cute guy headed our way. Never break the seal until you have to. I'm thinking Contestant Fireman didn't even have a seal to break! In fact, at this rate, I would bet he could pee out all the fires when he's on the job!

"Listen, I think I'm going to head out", I said, eyebrows raised in a giving up kind of way.

"Really? How come? Aren't you having a good time?" Contestant #11 asked.

That was the most he'd said in an hour!

"Well, honestly, I was, but I just feel like I've been doing all the talking, all the asking, and all the waiting."

"Really?" he asked, like what I was saying was unbelievable and news to him.

"Well, yeah. You haven't said much at all and you've been to the bathroom three times already. I'm starting to get a complex or something."

"Really? A complex?" he asked.

HELLO????? It's a figure of speech. You don't speak and all you do is pee!!!

"Well, not a *complex*, but I am running out of things to talk about which is really hard for me to do. I think we should just call it a night", I said.

I was totally surprising myself as the words came rushing out of my, often times, big mouth. I might have been surprising myself but I was feeling very proud and courageous, too. I didn't want to sit there anymore with someone who didn't speak so I was going to leave. That's that!

"I've been talking..." Contestant #11 tried to defend himself.

"Not really. You've been listening to me ramble in between your pee breaks and if I popped quizzed you on my rambling, I'm not even sure if you would pass because you have given me no indication that you have been the least bit interested", I defended back.

"I've been interested. I've been listening", he said.

"I guess I get the feeling people are listening when they chime in or add something or at lease nod along. Look, maybe it's just not happening for us and that's fine. I appreciate you driving over to me and I've enjoyed meeting you, but my jaw is tired from keeping this conversation going and I'm tapped out", I said with an apologetic smile.

"Okay, we can call it a night if you want", he politely, but kind of sadly, said.

We said our goodbyes, gave each other a quick hug and I seriously wondered if he was going to bolt around and run back in to pee again. I got in my car and left. I was going home to pee in my own bathroom and break the seal of this date. Contestant #11 was over.

Notes to self:
Talking.... is kind of essential during a blind date.
Too many a bathroom break can really leave a date at stake!

Contestant #12

How do you go on a date, meet someone for the first time, sit over a couple of drinks and not talk? I was still a little perplexed over that last date. I just couldn't figure Contestant #11 out. Maybe he was incredibly shy. Maybe I scared him- it has recently come to my attention that, apparently, I have the ability to scare a man. This is not something any man would ever admit, but usually when a guy shies away from me it's more than likely I scared him. How do I scare men? I have been told by many that I come across as a confident and strong woman. Why those two qualities would ever scare a man is beyond me. The funny thing is, I rarely feel strong and confident. It must be the way I do my eye make-up or something. So, clearly, I scared this guy off to the bathroom multiple times. Perhaps he really had to pee that frequently, perhaps, he was doing drugs, perhaps he was calling people on his cell phone. The question was, why did he keep returning? Who knows. Perhaps he just wasn't Mr. Right.

After a couple of weeks pondering over the latest unsuccessful attempt, I checked into my profile to see if anything was cooking. *Nothing.* Wow, when I first got on this thing, guys were hitting my profile all the time. *Now, nothing?* My profile used to be better than sliced bread. Now, it was more like stale bread. I was feeling like this was a do or die situation. If I didn't do something, this profile was going to die and I was never going to go on another date. I started browsing and clicking. I decided to keep the change of scenery to New Jersey for the 'what the hell' factor. There were a lot of guys in New Jersey! I didn't know any Jersey zip codes so I flew by the seat of my sweatpants and kept clicking. Then I found someone. He was very attractive. Not that I was surprised but it always surprises me to find very attractive men on these websites. This is going to come out very shallow and, possibly mean, although I really don't mean for it to sound this way. How come such good looking guys are on these websites? They must have girls gawking at them around every corner. Besides, girls have become so much more aggressive these days, I can't imagine that any of these gorgeous guys has never been approached. In fact, if I over think it, what's the matter with these guys anyway? Some of these guys are *not* about average like me. Some even put down *modeling* as a career. What guy model has a difficult time meeting women? So anyway, I was about to embark on Contestant #12. A dozen freaking guys. A dozen dates. A dozen stories.

Contestant #12 and I made easy contact through the dating website. It was immediate, which was a relief to me for the fact that I still wanted to be a little piece of the sliced bread. I didn't want to think or possibly accept that I was a stale slice already. Not stale, after only a dozen dates! That would suck.

He was another nice and attentive guy through the emails. He was also from New Jersey. Two nice looking guys from New Jersey. *Jon Bon Jovi--watch out! Just kidding. Not possible.* Anyway, Contestant #12 also agreed to do the driving over towards my way. I figured, since he was heading over the Tappan Zee Bridge, like Contestant #11, we might as well meet at my unlucky spot on the water. Why not shoot three for three. Maybe I didn't have a good vibe on the water. Maybe the view was killing my mojo, when in fact, I thought it should be adding to it since a good view always relaxes me.

It had been about three weeks since Non-Talker #11, and I felt it was safe to meet Contestant #12 at the same place. I was sure no one would remember me. It's not like Contestant #11 and I made a big conversational splash, drawing the attention of other patrons. If anything, just the opposite. Unless, maybe the bartender would remember me, the dumb redhead sitting there *again*, waiting for her date to return from the bathroom *again*. Nah. I doubted it. Although, when I used to bartend, that's the funny shit I used to pay attention to in between mixing drinks!

On a beautiful Friday night, I drove down to the waterfront restaurant and met Contestant #12 in the parking lot. The timing was great and neither of us had to wait for the other. *Maybe that was a good sign?* Contestant #12 was tall, maybe six foot four or so, he had olive skin tone, brown hair, deep brown eyes, and wore a little too much cologne, especially in the semi-humid weather on the water. That was okay, though because he was really nice to look at.

We casually walked towards the restaurant, using small talk as our security blanket to start the evening off right. Instead of having a drink inside, like with Contestant #11, we decided to enjoy the warm atmosphere on the outside deck. This was good because now no one would recognize me from a few weeks ago.

We looked around the outside deck, scoped the place out, saw that there were a few empty tables right by the water, and we walked over to a bar that resembled somewhat of a makeshift tiki hut.

"What are you going to drink?" I asked.

"I'm not really sure", he said "Maybe I'll do vodka tonight", he added insecurely.

When it was our turn to order, I stated that I would have a light beer please. Contestant #12 wanted vodka, but, apparently had no idea what he was asking for, talking about, or about to receive. I could name a half dozen vodka drinks off the top of my head this very second and, yet, I don't even drink the stuff. Why he was having such difficulty with this small task was beyond me.

"Uh, what kind of vodka do you have?" he inquired

"Absolute, Stoli, Kettle one, Grey Goose…..then we have flavored vodkas with berry or orange…" the bartender answered, waiting patiently for his order.

"Uh…I dunno…I'll have any one of those please", Contestant #12 replied.

The bartender looked at him with scrutiny, probably thinking and knowing that this guy had no idea what he was doing. It's not like you have to know what you're doing to order a drink, but most people pretty much know what to order for themselves and if there is any question, don't drink. It wouldn't be my first non-alcoholic date. At this point I was three sips into my beer.

"Well, how do you want it? Ice? No ice? Soda? Water? Fruit? What?" the bartender badgered.

"Just, whatever. Just some vodka in a cup, that's all", Contestant #12 stated hesitantly.

With a small headshake of disbelief, the bartender handed him a plastic cup, like one would drink from at a house party, filled 2/3's of the way with a clear, untitled, undressed vodka. *Eww.*

Okay, I needed to move past his drink order because the weather was warm and beautiful with a good sky. I always loved a good sky. It's always changing and keeps me completely mystified, like anything could happen. I was curious as to where this evening might be headed.

We found a little table right by the end of the deck with just a large rope separating us from the water. This might be good if one of us felt the need to jump in and drown ourselves but I was determined to remain optimistic. The place was a bit crowded and all the tables were filling up so I was relieved to have one of our own. I was also relieved that we were outside having cocktails in a more relaxed atmosphere than some of my other dates.

Contestant #12 and I chatted lightly over our drinks, learning a little bit about each other. He was still quite nice and had a gentle way about him. We watched some of the boats arriving into the docks and watched other people venturing out for a nice evening on their boats, something I always wished I could do, too. I never knew anyone with a boat.

Contestant #12 sipped his warm vodka and made the most unrecognizable face as the liquid burned south down his throat. *Why hadn't the guy gotten a couple of ice cubes?* I had just gotten a beer and that was pretty warm, too so I couldn't imagine trying to swallow harsh vodka on its own.

"Why don't you go switch your drink?" I asked.

"No, no, it's fine", he replied with a cringe.

"You don't seem to be enjoying it. At least grab some ice cubes so it's not so burny", I added.

"No, really, it's fine. I'm just not used to it, that's all."

"You don't normally drink vodka?" I asked him.

"Not really. I thought I would try something new", he said.

Huh.

I'm not sure I would try something that new if I were on a blind date, a far drive from home, in an area that I'm completely unfamiliar with. *Odd.*

"Okay. I'll go up there and get you some ice if you want. Maybe a lime or something", I said, trying to convince him.

"Really, I'm fine", he said with a reassuring smile, although I didn't believe him.

We spent some more time talking about work stuff, family stuff, and just general topics that I can't really remember. In fact, I can't remember much of the conversation because I was obsessed with his determination to drink that drink.

"Ugh! Gross!" Contestant #12 suddenly complained. He was swirling his warm vodka, sticking his pinky in it to fish something out.

"What's the matter?" I asked

"There's a bug in my drink!" he exclaimed.

I'm sure it wasn't alive at this point and probably died of alcohol poisoning the second it mistakenly dove into his beverage.

"Where?" I asked.

"Right there!" he pointed.

The gnat was no bigger than a grain of sand. I was never a big fan of the bug, any bug, they gross me out. *But, seriously, a gnat?* His finger was so big in that tiny cup, he was never going to fish it out.

He obsessed over it for a few minutes, obviously with no intention of ignoring it and possibly knocking it back with another sip of poison.

"Do you want me to try?" I asked, reaching for the cup. He handed the cup over, reluctantly, probably not thrilled that I was about to go fishing for it too. I gently held the cup in my left hand and tilted it while I steadily dipped my pinky nail towards the side and snatched up that little bugger in one swift movement. All gone. I have long nails, not too long, but long enough to scoop a bug, possibly unscrew a screw, or leave my mark on a fabulous back!

I digress.

"Okay, it's out." I said with confidence as a rumble of thunder vibrated in the background. I heard it because I love it, but there was music playing and lots of conversation all around us so it might have gone undetected but many at that moment.

"Thanks", he said, but I was pretty sure he wasn't going to continue drinking out of that cup. I was right. He went to the bar for another and brought back another for me. One would think he would have changed his cocktail choice, since he clearly wasn't enjoying the first one, but, no, he got the same damn thing! I wondered if he was trying to get drunk fast or just give himself quick alcohol poisoning.

Rumble! The clouds started rolling in over the sunset and the sky was gorgeous. The thick clouds were turning a rich shade of navy blue towards the north, while the sky towards the south was pink and orange cast by the sun setting in the west. I loved that kind of sky and could sit watching it until the whole thing eventually turned to darkness. Mesmerizing, is what I like to think of it. Maybe even inspiring, depending on my current mood.

I was getting lost in my thoughts over the potentially cool sky to come over the next few minutes, when a rumble came in louder and a bit more forceful.

"Oh my God! Was that thunder?" Contestant #12 asked.

"Yeah", I said. "It'll be cool to watch a storm roll in from out here, don't you think?" I added.

He shrugged and looked down at his drink. He took another sip and cringed again, his face contorting into strange shapes. We continued to chat and people watch and check out the boats coming in, obviously cautious of the oncoming storm. *BOOM!* Another crack and that one was accompanied by a flash of lightening over the hills. I was getting sort of excited because I had been down on this dock before with storms rolling in and it was definitely a sight to see.

"Maybe we should go inside if a storm is coming", Contestant #12 suggested somewhat nervously.

"Ohhh, not just yet", I said. "It's still a ways off and it's pretty to watch it roll in".

"Yeah, but there's lightening and we are right next to the water!" he claimed.

"True, but it's still a while away. We have some time. I just love it", I said.

"You love it? You love storms?" he asked incredulously.

"Well, yeah, they're kinda cool, especially when you can watch them approach, like now". It's not like I admitted I liked whips and chains. A simple storm was *not* that big of a deal in my mind. I don't know why it was apparently becoming such a big deal in his mind.

I was not moving. I had a good seat for this and I planned on being a great audience for the approaching festivities!

"I guess…." he said timidly *or* he thought I was just nuts!

Flash. Flash. Rumble….*BOOM!* Breeze…..

A couple of people boarded a little raft and started to head out to their boat.

"Oh my God! What are they doing?" Contestant #12 raised his voice.

"Probably going right out there to their boat", I replied.

"Do they know a storm is coming? Can't they see the lightening?"

BOOM! CRACK! Flash. Flash.

I wasn't sure, but I thought maybe this guy was petrified of thunder storms…. and gnats.

"They really shouldn't be out on the water in this weather. Look how small that little raft is! Where is their boat? How far out do they have to go? Oh Jeez!"

Flash. Flicker. *BOOM!*

The dark clouds were about to start rolling in on top of us but there was no rain yet, and therefore, I was sitting it out. He was shitting it out. I couldn't figure out what was more amusing at the moment, the storm or the guy! I had a front row seat to a variety show and everywhere I looked was entertaining!

"I'm sure they'll be fine", I said. "It's not even raining yet and there is a bunch of boats right out there. One of them probably belongs to the people in the raft", I added.

"Well, why would they *want* to go out on their boat with a storm coming?" he asked questioningly.

Clearly, #12 had no sense of adventure whatsoever. If I had a boat and a storm was rolling in, I would have my ass on there too! Not out in the middle of the sea, mind you. I'm not a fan of the Perfect Storm and I have a serious and psycho fear of floods and tidal waves. However, if the boat was so visible from the deck we sat on, how harmful could it be? I had other thunderstorm fantasies that do not include boats, but that really had nothing to do with this date anyway.

BOOM! CRACK! FLASH! Raaiiinnnn….Darn.

It was starting to rain so we gathered our things and moseyed on inside. There was a band setting up in the bar and Contestant #12 told the hostess that we would like a table. *Crap! The food thing again.* I was so content for the last hour watching the guy, the gnat, and the storm. Now it was going to be buzz killed by a meal.

We sat by the window, eating salad and some appetizers as the skies opened up and rained down hard on the deck we just sat on. The lightening lit up the sky and the thunder shook the small building. It was actually quite nice and I didn't mind it at all, until, I felt #12's hand on my leg! Not a brush of the knee, not even a hand on my knee. A hand on my *leg*. My *upper leg*. My *thigh*.

I guess his vodka kicked in and my drinking was done for the night. He moved even closer to me and draped his arm and hand around the back of my chair and made some chilling grumble in my ear when the rumble came in. Was he trying to *act* afraid of the storm? If he was trying to act afraid, it was weird, because a half an hour ago, I thought he really *was* afraid outside!

After the food portion of the date, the rain was letting up and the lightening and thunder continued southbound in the sky. Big drips landed on the deck as the only evidence of a previous storm. We finished our light meal and headed to the bar to check out the band. I wasn't sure how much longer this date would last and I still couldn't get an accurate vibe on the connection between us. It had been moving from one extreme to another and every time I thought I was getting a handle on this guy, he switched it up.

As the band was about finished setting up I knew they were familiar to me, I had seen them before. They played a lot of Led Zeppelin, Janis Joplin, The Stones, and The Doors. Pretty trippy, but really good. Contestant #12 ordered a beer for himself and tried desperately to convince me to have another as well. All I could think about was why he hadn't ordered a beer over an hour ago in the first place! *Why kill yourself with straight, warm vodka??* With his hand resting on my hips and the front of his body pressing up into the back of my body, I thought maybe it would be a better idea if I quit drinking for the night.

When I first met Contestant #12, I thought he was fairly attractive, clean, and gentlemanly. I was okay with the onset of this date until he freaked about the gnat in his weird, indecisive drink. As I was almost getting past that, he started freaking about the storm. I think I needed a date with a little more balls, although he was definitely finding them as the night wore on and they were pressing into my backside.

There were plenty of people around, for the band had a large following and a lively, fun crowd. The music was loud and rocking and Contestant #12 was all tipsy and swaying.

"Let's take a walk out onto the deck", he suggested. I just looked at him, trying to figure out if he was being serious. *Probably not a good idea.*

"C'mon", he coaxed and he took my hand and led me toward the door.

I tried to dissuade him, but since he was ahead of me leading the way with my hand in tow, and because the band was so loud, he really couldn't hear my mild protests. It's not like I was yanking back and screaming or anything because I was trying to be graceful and polite about it. It didn't work.

We strolled outside in the damp air, taking in the remnants of the recent storm. Nobody was outside anymore and the deck was quiet and fairly dark with the exception of the little decorative lantern lights circulating the perimeter of the deck still swaying from the earlier winds. Contestant #12 turned toward me.

"You know I'm going to kiss you now, right?" he said to me.

That was the most confident he'd been all night. I was trying to put some of the other idiosyncrasies out of my head and encourage myself to possibly enjoy what was coming my way.

"Are you?" I asked coyly with a mix of disbelief.

This guy was a hard read. I couldn't imagine he was going to go for it like he stated, only because he was such a wimp about the gnat not that long ago.

He leaned down into my face and planted one on my lips. For the first millisecond, I thought his lips were soft and gentle but then I gagged on his tongue, as he shoved it down my throat. He was taller than me and, therefore, had some height leverage on me which made it difficult for me to gasp any air. He had a good, strong hold around my lower back and the pressing of bodies started again, however I was the press-ee, not the press-er. It was a longer kiss than I had anticipated or even hoped for, if I had been hoping for one at all, which I was not quite sure I was. I finally had a miniscule opportunity to pull my head back, but, just my head because he still had a firm grip on my waist. My hands went up onto his chest to create some sort of barrier and my head went down.

Basically, he now had a view of the top of my hair. He tried another kiss. This time I had a little more time to veer off and I really discouraged his second attempt.

"I really need to get going", I said to him.

"Why? This is nice", he said back.

"I know. It was a very nice evening but I should really head out."

His squeeze got tighter around my middle.

"What if I wanna keep kissing you?" he prodded and teased.

"Probably not a good idea", as I was feeling suddenly suffocated by his cologne in the humidity. The thought of my throat being strangled by his tongue, made my stomach flop over my light dinner. This guy *might* have stood a *slim* chance if he had an *inkling* on how to kiss a woman! Nothing is better than a guy who can kiss. He could not.

He reluctantly lightened his hold around me and began leading me toward the exit of the deck. I felt so relieved and I didn't even care if he was pissed or disappointed. I wondered if he was one of those "player" types. Actually, I didn't really wonder that, I just figured his poisonous vodka drinks had gotten the better of him because he had really started off like quite the little Mary. I had never met a guy, friend or foe, who was afraid of gnats and lightening. Yeah, his bravery definitely came from the vodka because he already displayed what a wuss he was when he was whining over the snap, crackle, pop, of the thunderstorm.

We made it to our cars that were parked near each other and, amazingly, he leaned in quick for one more shot. My head dipped, turned, and serpentined itself through the small airspace into my pocketbook to find my keys.

I think that really ticked him off and he finished off with, "Nice meeting you, Jacey."

With that, he turned on his designer heel and walked off to his own car.

"Okayyy, bye", I called out, but that was really it.

Contestant #12 was over.

Notes to self:

Gnats are *not* killer bugs-even *I* know that!

Gagging someone with a tongue does not make one a good kisser.

A Daydream Dozen?

Asolid dozen. It just hung over me with invisible weight, like a storm cloud, dark and ominous. A dozen. As I drove home from one of my various mini car drives per day, I quietly pondered going for the baker's dozen, hoping maybe the infamously unlucky number 13 would have the reverse effect on me. *A dozen guys and not one connection? Not one spark? Not one ounce of potential?* That weighs a lot, invisible or not.

As I continued to drive along, thinking about each and every one, it forced my memory back to the day that I joined the online dating website just 7 years ago. I was so down and depressed, feeling like gravity was controlling the bright smile I once had. Everything was a chore, from getting out of bed in the morning, to chatting on the phone with basically anyone, to finding something to eat at night, alone. I was coasting through each day, not remembering what yesterday was about because everything seemed like one emotional blur after another. I was going through a grieving process that, apparently, divorced people go through just as someone would when there is a death. Death I was familiar with, but divorce, I was not and every day was another journey into the unknown, the unsure, and the unbelievable.

I bought self-help books to guide me through my daily feelings so I knew that each emotion was justified and verified through strange authors with PhD's. How had I ended up married with two kids and divorced all by the time I turned 30 years old? How, in all these months, years even, had I not been able to find someone who could make me happy again? Well, at least someone with a long-term goal in mind like myself. How is it that half the marriages all around me seemed so doomed so often, yet they go on to celebrate their 10th, 12th, 15th anniversaries? How come I only got a 5 year shot and then got hung out to dry? *Why?* I asked why every day, back then. *Why- was I not a good wife? Why-was I not a good lover? Why-was I not a good cook? Why-was I not a good anything? Why.*

But somewhere in this small journey of my life, I figured out why, at least for part of it. I was not supposed to be with my ex-husband any longer than it took to create two unbelievably, beautiful, special girls. I wasn't supposed to hit my 10th anniversary with him. I wasn't supposed to lean on him straight out of my parents' arms. *I just* wasn't supposed to because *it* wasn't supposed to be. When I figured that out and could stick with that indefinitely, I still needed to figure out *why* I hadn't found anyone else or *why* anyone else hadn't found me. Well, that's not entirely true, because in my heart I did, but of course, bad timing and lousy circumstances prevented my happiness tooth and nail!

A dozen damned dates. I supposed it was a huge feat for me to even get through a dozen dates, seeing as though I had never intended on going on even one until my mother, basically threatened my life. Maybe only a dozen dates in a span of seven years seemed pathetic but I like to think that the dating breaks were just as meaningful, if not, more important.

As I made a right turn onto my little dead end street and then made a quick right into my driveway, I spotted some slight movement out of the corner of my eye. I didn't see a car or a crowd so I wasn't sure what to focus on just yet. Blinking hard and squinting, I honed in on a handsome man who stood by the stone wall holding something close to his body. I looked at him strangely, with a very unattractive facial expression of frowning, skeptical eyes and a raised top lip. *Who was he? Where did he come from? Where was his car? Was he a psycho? Was he selling something? Wtf? More questions….they never end!*

I climbed out of my car, thankfully without my kids in tow, and approached the man. He was leaning against my stone wall in a somewhat relaxing way, kind of gazing at me as I got closer. His head was slightly tilted, holding up his body language in an easy going, confident sort of way. He had a faint grin across his lips as though he was finding mental amusement in my confusion and his eyes twinkled with knowledge of something to come.

"Hi", I said defensively. "Can I help you?"

"Hi Jacey", he said, like he knew me.

Immediately I felt strange inside. He knew my name, he knew where I lived, and he actually acted as though he knew *me*! Oh crap, had I done something completely stupid while I was out one night letting off a little bit of that divorce steam? Nah, I would've remembered *this* guy. I couldn't put my finger on it, but I swore he seemed very familiar to me, with a slight accent I couldn't quite detect. It was very subtle and I needed him to speak more to try and grasp it. Was it from another country, another state, someplace I had been before, or someplace that had visited me?

"I brought you something", he said as his faint grin turned into a lazy smile, as his lips curled up at the corners, revealing beautiful white teeth. He brought the item away from his chest and extended his beautifully, muscular arms forward towards me.

"What is this?" I asked, completely stumped and confused.

"What does it look like, silly. It's a can of flowers."

I reached out to meet his hands and he gently placed it in my hands while never taking his eyes off me. My eyes were locked into his, and I was drowning in the greenish hazel swirls as I tried to focus on the weight of the can in my hands. It wasn't any heavier than a full coffee can but I was so mesmerized by his beautiful eyes that I was having a hard time concentrating on the gift I was supposed to be holding.

Without blinking or flinching, this overwhelming calm came over me like a warm blanket as he leaned in and placed his free hands on my cheeks. This man, this stranger, this familiar soul tilted my chin up and kissed my lips with the utmost gentle passion I had ever experienced. His lips were soft and tender, which made mine feel and respond exactly the same. He kissed me like that's all he'd been doing his entire life. He hadn't ever forgotten the art of kissing and that it could be so much more than a suffocation or a theft. He kissed me for how ever long he stood there. I had no idea. Everything in my being had stopped except for this man before me. This beautiful man with tousled hair, bluish-green eyes, a body oozing a confident presence, smelling like clean soap, and a soft accent that was far from New York.

He raised his head and gently pulled his lips away, never taking his eyes away from mine. Then, he leaned towards me again and wisps of his breeze-blown hair brushed my cheek with a slight tickle. His closeness sent chills up and down my spine.

"That is how you should always be kissed", he whispered in my ear. His whisper was so soft but his words were so clear. I thought he would say more. I hoped.

I had been looking down, listening for more, staring at the simple, beautiful, pink flowers in a tin, coffee can. They smelled fragrant, and possessed a strong, colorful hue in such a plain can. I waited for more words and when no more came, I looked up. He was gone. The man was gone and I stood there holding my can of flowers. That was my Mr. Right.

Okay, okay, it was just a daydream, but it's my happy daydream that reminds my inner soul that maybe I shouldn't be settling. *Ever.* True, he wasn't real, just fragments of people all rolled up into a pretty little package who I believed could make me happy. I'm not delusional to think that any guy could be that perfect which is why he probably only exists in my head. He holds all the wonderful qualities of the small amount of men in my life that ever meant anything to me and some of the qualities that I can only hope for in a man someday. He is someone I conjured up in my mind to make me feel good when I was feeling truly down and discouraged. I don't believe in him but I would like to believe his message; *I am a can of flowers.....dammit!*

Perhaps, above?

When reflecting on my journey through divorce and online dating, I would be very inclined to label myself about average. But after my journey of divorce and online dating, I have decided that I am definitely not about average. I have grown in ways that I never thought I could. I got divorced at a young, unexpected age and that made me stronger, forced me to handle things on my own, and make decisions by myself, good or bad.

I dealt with infidelity, loneliness, and rejection. I dealt with a raging mother who wanted to cut off my ex-hole's balls and bronze them. I dealt with a caged lion of a lawyer who forced me into necessary but uncomfortable positions. I dealt with my father's sad disappointment and his attitude of staying fair even when everyone else wanted me to play dirty. I dealt with two babies who needed me every second of every day, including the nights I rocked in the rocking chair as they battled fever, new teeth, and ear infections. I dealt with biased friends who only wanted the best for me and couldn't understand my motives for letting my ex-hole try to be a good father. I dealt with the daily idea of being single and trying to get myself out there again. I dealt with internet dating that paired me up with the likes of people whom were strange, shy, aggressive, harmless, and just plain odd. I dealt with my self-esteem after a few heartfelt break-ups. I dealt. I dealt with the cards that were dealt to me.

The only thing that kept me consistently grounded was that I had two small children. All I have done is strive to be a good mother, a combination of the mother and father, who raised me. I have made it my priority to ensure their happiness, health, and education. Is it the Beaver Cleaver household? Hell no, not even close. I would describe it more as a Mermaids kind of household, and I'm Cher. I *am* a single mom.

For any other single mom's out there….enough said! I do my best and I still seem to find myself two steps behind, but I always hope to catch up, eventually.

I became an about average teacher….is there such thing? No teacher is about average on any day. I shape young minds for God sake. How can that be about average? I don't stare at a computer screen or sit in a cubicle or schmooze for a promotion or even wipe somebody's ass. I teach! I teach small children! I teach them everything that their own parents can't. I teach small children things that their parents *don't*! I have my summers off and I get granted the occasional snow day but all year long, I work my ass off!

Lastly, a size 12? Yes, my theory is that size 12 is more than about average because it's *never* in stock. Most women would like to *believe* that they are a size 2 or a size 4, but if that's the case, why are those the clothes hanging on the rack at the end of the day? I can't even get my ankle through a size 2! I patiently look for a 12 and, more often than not, I am jumping from the size 4 to the size 16 with nothing in the middle to choose from. *Whose average now, girls!!!*

I didn't sit at my desk and decide to write that I was fabulous and my life was going exactly as planned, because I'm not fabulous and neither is my life. I didn't sit at my desk with some self-righteous attitude, lying to myself about how I've overcome all of my obstacles and I'm a better person for it because, I haven't. I didn't sit at my desk and feel happy that I was even writing this book because I would've rather been spending my time with someone a little more special then my damn computer again. However, I did feel that the time on my computer reflecting on this journey had been full of more quality experience than the countless hours I spent clicking and browsing blind dates, trying to find Mr. Right. About average? Nah. Above average? Yeah, perhaps. How about…… just normal?

A Baker's Freebie

I had an astrology party not long ago with a fabulous woman who has been to my house many times. She has given me many readings using tarot cards throughout this entire ordeal. The last time she saw me, my reading had changed significantly since I was 30 years old. The astrologist had confirmed that I reached personal strength, that I felt secure, that I will gain what I wish because I believe. She saw that people had entered my life from my past, some who have helped my self-esteem, like my very first boyfriend. He is one man who, besides my father, has seemed to have loved me unconditionally all these years and although he is married with children, he has always taken the opportunity to point out to me how loved I will always be. He will also confirm that the men that have hurt me are 'tools'.

Some might see that as "crossing the line" on his part, and it probably is to some extent and often times makes me feel more than weird inside. However, the magic it has lit in my heart about how I should view myself is invaluable. That is the only line I *ever* crossed with him.

Another had re-entered my life, Break #3. Where would it head, no one knows. Maybe nowhere. Judging from my past, Break #3 always headed towards heartbreak so being cautious would be a good place to start. We had been in touch for some time because I decided to reach out to him a bunch of months ago. *Why would I do that on purpose?* I needed some peace.

In the recent past, my ex-hole had chosen to get remarried to the girl that scapped him up while our bed sheets were still warm. He gave me the impression that he wanted to come home at one point a few years back, and tried to convince me that he was a changed man.

"Do you think we could ever be happy again?" he asked while dragging on a cigarette outside on the deck.

It could be my chance. A second chance. A new beginning. A family torn apart and put back together. What were the odds on that happening?

"No" I said sadly, shaking my head after a long pause.

"But why? I've changed" he stated somewhat insecurely.

"Because I could never ever trust you again. That's why."

"I'm not the same person I was, Jacey. I'm not."

"I can't do it. I can't wake up every morning wondering if you're just gonna change your mind again."

Ironically, I have done that with every relationship ever since.

That was it. That's where it ended. I knew that I never wanted to go backwards with this man again. I never wanted to risk being hurt by him again. I would never trust him again. He never even said he was sorry for what he did to me, to our children, to our families.

I knew I could never be happy with someone who had hurt me so deeply to the core of my being. Especially someone who never even had the thought cross his mind to say he was sorry. Just apologize. Make amends. Take responsibility. I was done.

I'm not really sure if he wanted to come home for me, the girls, or simply because I was crying about someone else that broke my heart. He wriggled into that part of the conversation saying just the right things like 'losing you was my biggest mistake' and 'that guy will realize it one day, just like I did'.

I made a decision at that very moment that I was not going to ever settle again. Not with the dates and not even with my ex-husband. He lied to me and betrayed me and to invite him back into my life would be unthinkable. If he chose to apologize, I would have liked to be able to forgive and move forward with my own peace, but he didn't. So, he decided to get married to someone else and have our children break the news to me. *That was mature!*

It still pissed me off to no end. I spent an entire season of fall being pissed off and made a personal decision to let one off the hook. Break #3 was going to be forgiven for causing me heartbreak even though he would never actually know that. I just didn't have the energy to have so much anger in me and I really felt that my ex-hole deserved all of it at the time. I always knew Break #3 was a good man and he probably never meant to hurt me in the first place. *Forgive? Yes. Forget? Probably never, but I would try to make the effort.*

So I sent Break #3 an impromptu Happy Birthday message, thinking that would give me enough peace with him. I reached out, I was nice, and that was that. Not really. Although I never even expected a response from him, we somehow got caught in the web of text messages for many months. Finally, it graduated to phone calls and, honestly, it was like we never skipped a beat. I knew that the natural course of action would be to get together eventually, maybe to test the waters of being in the same vicinity of each other. The catch was, would he have the guts to match mine?

After some gentle prodding, on my part, we agreed to get together and have a little dinner. I saw his new house which gave me a sense of comfort, knowing where he was and how he was living. Not that I'm going to turn into some crazy street fair stalker, but just the small fact of knowing was okay with me. I had remembered when buying a house was an idea he had, so I was feeling really happy for him and the great strides he had made to move forward with his life after his divorce.

I was a little nervous about seeing him again, however, our plans were so last minute that I was rushing to get ready and get there. I really had no time to worry about my worries. I took a record fast shower, applied my make- up and blew my hair out upside down which causes wild waves and curls. Not ideal for my first choice of pressured style, but I was in a serious time crunch. I threw on Capri jeans and a black tank. Casual, but enough skin showing.

I found his house without a problem and walked right in like I owned the place. Keys on the kitchen table, flip flops slid off in the corner of the kitchen, and Break #3 walking around the corner without a shirt. *What? Not fair.* He hadn't heard me pull up or come in because he had already begun cooking out on the grill in the back. He casually slipped on a shirt and gave me the grand tour of his house. I really did feel happy for him. It was a nice house and seemed just perfect for him. Sadly, I did find myself glancing around for certain, familiar things, like particular poems or paintings but there was nothing on the walls except a clock and a mirror. Hopefully he saved my hand-made gifts somewhere, or that would surely have broken my heart to pieces. I silently convinced myself that they were well-protected in the basement. Even if they weren't.

He cooked me steak, which is an old pastime of our last stint and we sat and chatted for hours out on the patio. The backyard was peaceful with trees surrounding the dead-end property. Music played from inside, the beer bottles were cold, and the atmosphere felt relaxing. This time, there was no awkwardness, no stress, no tension, except for maybe the bats that were flying way above in circular motions as the sun sunk. We sat outside through dusk and watched the bats circle above until I couldn't take the idea that they would swoop down at any moment and get lost in my crazy hair! We finally decided to move inside when the mosquitoes began feasting on my legs. *Mine, not his.*

We sprawled out on the floor looking at photos of kids and vacations. We sipped on beer and played guess-the- hair band-game on the radio. We told each other stories, teased and laughed. I was even asked if I would be okay to drive home. *Three times.* I was fine to drive home and I had no intention of pretending I wasn't. *Sometimes I wish I did pretend, though.*

When the evening had begun winding down, we hugged goodbye, with a small peck on the cheek. Could I have done more? *Hell yeah!* After three years, he looked great to me. I was more concerned about the 7 pounds I packed on since then. Anyway, I wasn't about to rock the lifeboat, so I just displayed confidence and comfort rather than neediness and insecurity.

He insisted I text him when I got home safely and at that moment we both decided that it went very okay. To me, it felt close to perfect. It was easy and in sync, like three years never went by. It was relaxing and comfortable, like we've been doing that forever. And, it was full of flirty, playful, mildly, sexual tension, that will always encumber the two of us. Even though nothing happened besides a hug and a peck on the cheek, knowing that we could have thrown each other down on the kitchen table at any second was a good feeling for me! Of course, I could've been reading too much into it and I could've been the only one with the kitchen table fantasy, while he might have been fantasizing about throwing me out the door instead, who knows! But, needless to say, I thought it went really well and I would like to think the number 13 is just a myth of being unlucky, because I didn't really feel unlucky at that moment. I felt pretty okay.

Although I haven't heard from him in a while, I'm still wishing on my stars that the number 13 will never turn unlucky for me. However, I'm sure he is having some huge mental argument with himself about all the reasons why I'm probably not a good idea. He'll come around eventually. If not to get together again, than at least to keep in touch and that will be something I'll just have to learn to accept from him, and from life. I know deep down inside that he will forever shy away from the very things I tend to lunge at. While we have a small gray area of deep understanding and agreement between us, he will probably never be ready for the things that I have been ready for all this time. Maybe I should be content that my last date was #13 and it went well, even if that's all it goes. Deep in my heart, I knew I could have made him happy if he had ever let me.

My cards viewed him as the King that I must have patience for. I'm not sure what he is King of. *Maybe my heart? Maybe his house? Maybe the gym?* All I know is that patience is definitely not my virtue, nor was it ever, but, perhaps, it's time for me to start exploring some patience and see what path my life may take or could take - King or no King. I would prefer to view him as my 'Baker's Dozen' and not necessarily a 'King'. To me, 'King', refers more to power, rules, royalty and might be quite a strong title for this portion of my story, so, instead, I will entitle him Date #13, the Baker's Dozen. Maybe the unlucky 13 *is* just a myth and my dating exploration and quest for sweet love will change that! Or maybe I just got a free good date out of this crazy experience, like getting a free bagel! Maybe my freebie was the reward I got for dating all those other Contestants! I'll take the freebie and end it on a good note!

I really don't feel the need to mentally argue with myself over all of my analyzing, but I think it's time I just hang back with some newly discovered patience and see where the path leads. Probably not that far, because there is only so much patience I can muster up for one human being!

I am the Empress and I am strong and confident, two things I was definitely not when I embarked on the dating world. In fact, I'm not 100% sure I feel strong and confident most of the time. *I try. I put up a good front.* However, no one really sees me when the house is sleeping and quiet…. I would like to truly be this way one day without the front, and, for that, I'll have to muster up the patience I need for *myself.*

My children are my Center, my core, my being and I would have it no other way, so no matter what path I take, who I date, where we live, what I teach, my children are with me every step of the way to continue to enlighten me with the pure innocence of everything life has to offer. I only hope one day I can offer them the type of family life I grew up with, even if it's just in the most minuscule amount. But kids, they don't know any differently unless they've had something to compare it to. Maybe one day.

Now, I can understand that many may think the cards are a whole bunch of bullshit, and that's okay. I never had a strong religious background so somewhere along my crazy paths of life, I found a little peace in the cards. The astrologist doesn't sit behind her crystal ball, predicting my future. It's more or less a confirmation of the paths your life has been taking and most likely will. They make me believe and they have always made sense to me as long as the person reading them believes and makes sense of them, too. The cards are not bullshit to me, they are like a light at the end of each tunnel, letting me know that my life and my experiences are not bullshit at all. They go along perfectly with my strong belief in angels and guidance. My brother, my Nannie. They know what I'm doing even if I don't have a clue!

Gunshot

My profile. I am shutting it down for a while. I know myself, and I know my Mr. Right is not in a thumbnail photo with his likes and dislikes plastered all over the screen. He is not standing in his photo topless, flexing his arms and abs in a mirror while he snaps pictures of himself with his cell phone. Mr. Right is not the daydream guy either because he *is* a daydream and we all have our own, I just chose to share! I'm not insane because I daydream about what kind of person I wish for in my life. I have discovered that I am picky, I won't settle, not for myself, not for my girls. Maybe through this whole journey, I have learned that I might rather be alone than settle. I can accept flaws and quirks, and a little OCD behavior. Lord knows, I suffer from all that, too. But settle? That's not necessarily accepting.

My profile could never truly reflect the person I am, or the person I've grown into or even the person I strive to be. Men will always see me as 'about average' on the computer screen. I will never be blonde, a size 2, or any sort of arm candy. I will never claim to love camping or surfing or jazz. Honestly, I can bike and enjoy it and I might like a hike with the right person, especially if there is a beautiful view of something in the end. But camping? Too many bugs and animal sounds…and where would I pee? Surfing? Not with my constant fear of floods and tidal waves! Jazz? I can't find a beat, sorry.

I will never settle into a second date when I know there is no click, or I might be gagged by a bad kisser who has an uncontrollable tongue, or sit humiliated because someone doesn't have any manners and drowns himself in a plate of ranch dressing. I have found an inner strength and power thanks to my dating experiences that has taught me that I don't have to say yes to a kiss or another drink or even a sit-down dinner with my nipple being pointed out as a doorway to one's apartment. That I don't have to question myself when the rocker-wannabe-trucker dumps me over the internet, and that I don't have to stick around with someone that doesn't want to talk to me, or possibly can't talk at all.

Did I think I was going to die back in the beginning? Hell yeah. Did I die on the dates? Not really. Maybe just severely wounded at times. Could I possibly die at the idea of more online dating? More than likely. To me, online dating was worse than having my mother point her emotional gun in my back. To me, online dating was like being a bullet and having the trigger fire you out into the open airspace. There you are, looking for some target while traveling at light speed, hoping you hit something, hoping the person that fired you out there had enough sense to have decent aim.

I think I'm quite done 'online'. Truthfully, I would rather meet a guy 'online' at the bank, or 'online' at a carnival ride, or 'online' at the concession stand at one of our kids' games. These are really the only types of lines I want to be on right now.

So maybe the clicking and the browsing and the winking worked for many, with plenty of marriages to prove the online dating theory of success, but I don't think it's my cup of tea. In fact, I don't even care for tea! I find it bland and watered-down. I'm more of a coffee girl, just a little stronger, maybe a little more awakening.

My life is full. My girls keep my heart full, my parents keep my confidence full, my friends keep my smile full, and my career keeps my mind full. That's it for now. About average. No. Above average. Yes, perhaps I am above average. I would like to believe that I am the pink flower in the plain, tin can that is growing everyday and blooming all the time. Do I still have the occasional pity party for myself? *Hell yeah!* Who can do that better than yourself! My life is full but I still find time to cry. Even though I have such a full life, sometimes I still get full of a whole lot of lonely.

I'm thrilled and grateful my mom stuck that gun in my back and forced me to get out there in cyberspace and I'm glad I found the courage to follow through. She stuck that gun in my back to get me out of my pajamas, to get me to stop living in a tissue box, to get me to start enjoying my children, to get me to lose some weight, change my look a little, find some confidence. My mom may have never understood exactly what dark place I was rotting in, but she understood how to get me out. How? I have a spiritual idea....

My profile had over 13,500 hits and I managed to finagle just a dozen dates out of that. That might not be sliced bread to many, however, its a dozen crumbs I gathered…all by myself. Perhaps, I've grown? Perhaps I could be above average? Maybe.

Perhaps I've hit the 7th inning stretch or a 7 year itch or, maybe, after 7 years, it's time I take one final break…. and break up with my online relationship.

Notes to self:
Bury profile in cyberspace cemetery.
Log off.

Epilogue

Status Update

"Still hanging in there and doing just fine."

I didn't go back into my rotting hole, the place I might have been in after my separation. I didn't go back on the matchmaking website, the place that I didn't succeed on after my divorce. And, I didn't find my true love, yet. I reflected, I remembered, I learned, and I wrote.

I reflected. I reflected on my hurt in the beginning of my divorce and how unfair I still thought it was. My head spun with second-guessing and my heart forced me to give myself a little pat on the shoulder. I patted myself for learning how to pay bills on my own, hang pictures on my own, landscape on my own, juggle 2 children on my own, hold down a job on my own, for trying…anything, on my own. Whatever I couldn't handle, I had my parents and friends to thank for that.

I remembered. I remembered the dates. The ridiculous dates, the dates that taught me how to date again, the dates that reminded that I hated dating! The dates that inspired me to share funny stories, the dates that reminded me that I needed the occasional breaks from dating. I remembered how scared I was and how insecure I felt when I started dating again. I remembered the mental fights I would have with my computer screen, wanting so much more than what was being offered to me through the website I established a relationship with. I remembered that I just wanted *more*.

I learned. I learned so much about life and about myself. Not everything, but enough to know that life isn't ever exactly what one signs up for and that one can really rise to the occasion when life backs you into a corner. I learned that the dates were important for my personal growth, but the relationships in between were even more important because those were the ones that forced me to feel again, to love again, and to hurt again…which still makes me human, something I questioned every now and then.

I learned that maybe this *isn't* the life I signed up for, but it's mine and it was time to make the most of it. I learned to say what I wanted, when I wanted it. I learned that life is too damn short to let a minute pass by without telling someone how you feel. Is that a big chance in life? *It sure is*. But, I would rather my feelings be known than wandering around with a big "what if" cloud hanging over my head.

I wrote. I wrote and I wrote and I wrote which is something I have never done before. I can write a damn good letter, a beautiful poem, and an excellent invitation but I had never ventured into Book Land. *Very scary*. After hearing the reactions of my friends while retelling my dating experiences, crying on their shoulders after heartbreaks, and getting the 'chin up' lecture from them, I felt like maybe I had something to say. I didn't know what I wanted to say or how I wanted to say it, but I definitely had *something* to say! So, I sat, writing it all down for others to read, giggle, cry, scoff at, whatever. I wrote without a plan of attack or even a clue of how it should be done. *Was there a way or a plan to write about your life?* I just started and figured that the way it came out was the way it was supposed to be written.

Eventually I learned about a new place to connect with people. It was another place where I was becoming "friended", another website that I graduated to after the matchmaking one. My new friendly website was another sense of personal growth, where I could post daily updates about myself, add photos, chat with friends, play games, take stupid quizzes, and… become in touch with all kinds of people, *old and new!!*

Every day I checked this new found website and became re-friendly with many people from my childhood. It was nice to hear from people, see their pictures, their kids, and learn about what's been going on with them over the years. Usually, it dwindled after the initial 'hey, how are ya', but the "friendship" remains in the little window to the left of the computer screen.

I also became re-friendly with people from my high school years. This was funny to me because I was a complete rebel in high school and never went beyond the small, delinquent group of friends I had. We were part of the 'Smoking Section' in one of the most elite high schools in the country! Half the time, we barely made it to class and I spent every summer in summer school making up the classes I had made no time for during the regular school year. Even gym! However, it was great to be in touch with so many people, realizing that they too, had had much personal growth and weren't the snobby bitches and idiots I originally thought they were back in the 80's! I had upper classman friending me, lower classman friending me, and even people whose asses I kicked in the bathroom and got suspended for friending me. I figured, *what the hell!* Let's all be friends because life is too *damn* short!

Through my daily status updates, I found myself LOL (laughing out loud), a lot. I was intrigued by private messages, instant messages, and regular posts for all to see. I found my sense of humor again which seemed to open doors for others to be intrigued by me. Was there anyone intrigued by me? Yes, there were...

Whatever website I decide to embark on will continue to be a new experience for me. The dating has gotten easier but there are still plenty of idiots out there. I'm still secretly hoping that not *everyone* is an idiot and I *know* there are some very good men out there. Sometimes I feel like I have a whole plate of everything but a whole bowl of nothing, yet there always seems to be *something* cooking! At least I know I'm *not* rotting in a corner of my house, withering away in a self-absorbed depression. There is life after a divorce. *I'm hanging in there and doing just fine...*

Status Update

"I'll let ya know....because, ya never know..."

Glossary (in my own terms)

<u>ADD</u>- Attention Deficit Disorder.

<u>Appy</u>- A completely ridiculous shortening of a perfectly normal word. Appetizer.

<u>Arm Candy</u>- Usually a small, petite, beautiful woman that looks as good on a man's arm as a Prada bag looks on a woman's arm.

<u>Baggage</u>- Some people might consider past experiences the extra stuff that they have to lug around from relationship to relationship.

<u>Bert</u>- Ernie's counterpart.

<u>Breaking the Seal</u> - First pee of the night, usually leading to many pee breaks and interrupting fun moments while waiting on line for the busy bathroom.

<u>Closure</u>- Some mental game one plays within themselves that they are ready to move on from whatever experience they just ended.

<u>Cricket</u>- My conscience.

<u>Dig</u>- Like

<u>Ex-Hole</u>- My clever combination of Ex-husband and Asshole.

<u>Fabuloutize</u>- A word I created as a verb; to make fabulous!

<u>Flag</u>- Warning.

<u>Friended</u> – to become friends with someone.

<u>Insurance Policy</u>- A sure thing (hook-up) No strings attached, no questions asked.

<u>Jazzed</u>- Excited.

<u>LOL</u>- Laughing out loud

<u>MoJo</u>- Personal magnetism, surrounding charm.

<u>OCD</u>- Obsessive Compulsive Disorder.

<u>Perch</u>- To sit poised on a barstool or semi-uncomfortable chair that is typically too small for one's ass.

<u>Perm</u>- A 1980-1990's hairstyle of tight curls made permanent in your head with toxic chemicals. AKA- big hair.

<u>Players</u>- Men who play on your feelings, your sexuality, or your vulnerability. They play you like a game and you're so smitten, you have no clue and then get hurt.

<u>Presence</u>- When a person displays a strong sense of confidence which is felt by those all around.

<u>Press-ee</u>- The person getting pressed upon.

<u>Profile</u>- A certain amount of semi-personal information describing yourself in the square space of a computer screen.

<u>Real Estate</u>- Empty space, with or without stools, at a bar.

<u>Roost</u>- To sit where you are and enjoy the vibe you're in without feeling the need to move anytime soon.

Serial Daters- People who constantly date, just to say they're dating. It doesn't matter who they date, where they date, or what they date.....they just MUST be dating to say they're dating.

Set-ee- One of the two people being set-up.

Sexting- Text messaging yourselves through sexual acts. Often difficult to do one-handed...

Schmooze- Mingle, socialize, network.

Stray- To cheat, to move off of the faithful path and stray towards temptation.

TMI- Too Much Information (usually stated as a statement)

Tool- Besides the obvious screwdriver or power drill, a tool can also refer to one as being an IDIOT!

Tourette's Syndrome- A nervous disorder characterized by involuntary movements.

Unfriend- To not be friends with someone anymore.

WTF- What the Fuck? (usually stated as a question)

Wuss- Wimp.

86 – All out of; Get rid of.

My parents:
I wish I could invent words that go beyond 'thank you'
because saying thank you never seems like enough.
I love you.

My Daughters:
I hope you know that you will forever be my first
loves. You fill my heart unconditionally.
Everyone else ~ will always come second.

My Friends:
My girls, my sisters. I am nothing without the smile you
put on my face and the laughs you create in my core.
'Ya know I love ya more than my luggage!'

"This is the story of my life and I write everyday and I hope
you're by my side, when I'm writing the last page"
~Bon Jovi~

Not….the end.